# LAMENTATIONS

# By Daniel Berrigan

## Prose

*The Bride: Essays in the Church*
*The Bow in the Clouds*
*Consequences, Truth and*
*Love, Love at the End*
*They Call Us Dead Men*
*Night Flight to Hanoi*
*No Bars to Manhood*
*The Dark Night of Resistance*
*America Is Hard to Find*
*The Geography of Faith* (with Robert Coles)
*Absurd Convictions, Modest Hopes* (with Lee Lockwood)
*Jesus Christ*
*Lights On in the House of the Dead*
*The Raft Is Not the Shore*
(with Thich Nhat Hanh)
*A Book of Parables*
*Uncommon Prayer: A Book of Psalms*
*Beside the Sea of Glass: The Song of the Lamb*
*The Words Our Savior Taught Us*
*The Discipline of the Mountain*
*We Die before We Live*
*Portraits: Of Those I Love*
*Ten Commandments for the Long Haul*
*Nightmare of God*
*Steadfastness of the Saints*
*The Mission*
*To Live in Peace: Autobiography*
*A Berrigan Reader*
*Stations* (with Margaret Parker)
*Sorrow Built a Bridge*
*Wheron to Stand (Acts of the Apostles)*
*Minor Prophets, Major Themes*
*Isaiah: Spirit of Courage, Gift of Tears*
*Ezekiel: Vision in the Dust*
*Jeremiah: The World, the Wound of God*
*Daniel: Under the Siege of the Divine*
*Job: And Death No Dominion*
*Wisdom: The Feminine Face of God*
*Lamentations: From New York to Kabul and Beyond*

## Poetry

*Time without Number*
*Encounters*
*The World for Wedding Ring*
*No One Walks Waters*
*False Gods, Real Men*
*Trial Poems (with Tom Lewis)*
*Prison Poems*
*Selected & New Poems*
*May All Creatures Live*
*Block Island*
*Jubilee*
*Tulips in the Prison Yard*
*Homage (to G. M. Hopkins)*
*And the Risen Bread*

## Drama

*The Trial of the Catonsville Nine*

# LAMENTATIONS

From New York to Kabul and Beyond

## DANIEL BERRIGAN

## with art by
## Robert McGovern

Foreword by Colleen Kelly

Lanham, Maryland
Chicago, Illinois

SHEED & WARD
Lanham, Maryland
Chicago, Illinois

Published by Sheed & Ward
an imprint of Rowman & Littlefield Publishers, Inc.
4720 Boston Way
Lanham, MD 20706

12 Hid's Copse Road
Cumnor Hill, Oxford OX2 9JJ, England

Printed in the United States of America

Cover and interior design: Madonna Gauding

Library of Congress Cataloging-in-Publication Data Available

ISBN: 1-58051-129-5

*To*
*"September Eleventh Families for Peaceful Tomorrows"*
*Nobility and courage*
*open*
*another way*
*than war*


✦   ✦   ✦

*It is good*
*to hope*
*in silence*

*for*
*the saving help*
*of God (Lamentations 3, 6)*

# Contents

# Foreword

Growing up in an Irish Catholic family is a lesson in storytelling. My family has a story for everything. I suppose this has helped teach all of us about life. Isn't that what stories really set out to do? Teach. Give meaning to events and feelings that we may otherwise find difficult to describe or understand. It seems appropriate then that I begin with a story about one of the many lessons I've learned, and continue to learn from the death of my brother.

Bill Kelly, Jr. is his name. I can't write "was" his name. Bill Kelly, Jr. is his name in death as it is in life. Billy didn't work at the World Trade Center, he just happened to be there on September 11, 2001, attending a breakfast conference at Windows on the World. Perhaps this is the fact I selfishly lament the most, a cruel twist of fate. Why was *he* there that particular day? Because I live and work in New York City, my sisters were calling me that morning to check on Bill. I kept reassuring them he must be fine, he worked miles away from the burning towers. False assurances; he was there. His last message at 9:23 a.m. said he was trapped on the 106th floor. He is gone and we have nothing physically of him, except our own visceral response to the stories of his life.

When my brother was in college, he took a course on "Death and Dying." One of the required books was entitled *Lament for a Son* by Nicholas Wolterstorff. This story chronicles a father's thoughts and feelings about the sudden, tragic death of his son as a young adult. When the course finished, my brother gave the book to his girlfriend at the time, whose own brother was dying a tragic yet slow death from AIDS. He asked her to give the book to her mother because he felt it might help her mom as a parent dealing with the impending loss of her child. Bill's girlfriend never gave her mother the book. Instead she saved it, long after my brother and she parted ways. Over ten years now. But on September 15 she did give that book to a mother in the depths of sorrow . . . my mother.

She doesn't know why she never gave her own mother the book. She doesn't know why she never threw it away. She wasn't really sure my mother would now want the book. But what a gift. Inside its aging pages my brother's handwritten notes cover the margins, his own thoughts and feelings about a young man dying much too soon. Bill even highlighted passages he thought especially important. My mother cherishes this precious gift. It echoes her lament for her son. After all, it is my brother's story too, with his own running commentary. How many mothers are so lucky? How many mothers are so sad?

What then of this story? The lament of one man expressed as a written tribute to his son, resounding now within my mother and father, marched toward full chorus in this sorrow-trodden world.

Were it not for Dan's beautiful poetic verse, I'm not sure I could have finished the book you now hold. It is painful to read. I suppose that most will find this so, not just those of us who lost someone they love so fiercely on September 11th. Why does it hurt? Its raw indictment of our culture's role in the violence is laid bare. My first impulse is to disagree, to take offense.

> God marked for destruction the wall of daughter Zion,
> Stretched out the measuring line—a hand brought ruin
>     but did not relent—
> Brought grief on wall and rampart till both succumbed.
> (2:8)

and

> Through the sin of which she is guilty, Jerusalem is defiled.
> All who esteemed her, think her vile now that they have
>     seen her nakedness.
> She herself groans and turns away. (1:8)

My brother was not a part of this. He was a kind man, loving to so many. What then was the sin so great as to warrant the horrible death of thousands? This isn't my idea of a loving and merciful God, or a world of beauty. But then I realize how much I've missed the point. It's not about Bill, or me, or you, but all of us collectively. How are we, as a people, the contemporary counterparts to the biblical crisis retold in *Lamentations?* If we are truly interested in searching for the answer why, then the hurts of the entire world must be exposed. Like doubting Thomas's, we must probe the wounds for ourselves, slowly, deeply. We must look into the pit of Ground Zero's all over—New York, Kabul, Zion—and let our tears flow.

Father Michael Lapsley helps a great deal here. He is an Anglican priest whose two arms were blown off by a letter bomb sent to him because of his work in South Africa against apartheid. He now heads the Center for the Healing of Memories in Capetown. When the Truth Commission was taking place in South Africa, Michael realized that there would be thousands who would never have the chance to tell their stories of terror and grief. He knew firsthand that public acknowledgment and memory of wrongs committed is the first step to healing. He was the first person to make me shudder when he looked me straight in the eye and said, "I am so sorry this has happened to you." He was the first person I've heard speak about restorative justice. It's not enough to simply return the bicycle you've stolen and say you're sorry. You should buy a new tire for the wronged also. He was the only person to tell me that I can't forgive my brother's murderers, only my brother can do that. I can only forgive for wrongs committed against me: the immeasurable loss of Bill in my life. Still, I need someone from al-Qaida to say, "I'm sorry." Thousands of families do. Just as certain, other parts of the world await their apology for harm done them: Kabul, San Salvador, Rwanda.

The connective theme to *Lamentations* surely lies in its universality. To grieve, to wrong and be wronged is to be human. The anguish, the moaning, the flow of tears; there is not disparity regarding fixture in place or time. *Lamentations* calls for humility, recognition of our humanness, then justice for all.

> God has broken my teeth with gravel, pressed my face in
>     the dust.
> My soul is deprived of peace, I have forgotten what
>     happiness is.
> I tell myself, my future is lost, all that I hoped for from
>     God. (3:16–18)

The imagery couldn't conjure up anything besides submission. To juxtapose this picture with that of Uncle Sam, rolling up his sleeve, fists clenched, ready for the fight, is quite a contrast. Where is our memory? What have we learned? Has our country squandered the chance of connectedness with the majority of the globe? Father Berrigan's thoughts on this are most provocative, but then, isn't that the purpose of prophetic prose?

My husband and our two older boys have been reading *The Lord of the Rings* series by J. R. R. Tolkien for years now, usually right before bedtime. Again, a story, imagined by a man of vision. But again, a story that teaches its readers young and old. Here we see Frodo, scared and frightened, lamenting missed opportunities to kill Gollum and thus expediently remove the source of his legitimate fears.

"O Gandalf, best of friends, what am I to do? What a pity that Bilbo did not stab that vile creature, when he had a chance!"

Pity? It was pity that stayed his hand. Pity and mercy: not to strike without need.

Said Frodo, "I can't understand you. Do you mean to say that you and the Elves have let him live on after all these horrible deeds? Now at any rate he is as bad as Orc, and just an enemy. He deserves death."

"Deserves it! I dare say he does. Many that live deserve death. And some that die deserve life. Can you give it to them? Then do not be too eager to deal out death in judgement. For even the very wise cannot see all ends."

Would that it could all be so straightforward. Good and evil, an axis for each. The bin Laden's of the world as neatly columned as the Gollum's. Tolkien reminds us there's a lot more to it. Dan's poetic reflections do the same.

Colleen Kelly
July 1, 2002

# Acknowledgments

This page invites an apothegm or two.

A tree stands on its roots. So does a book; its root is friendship. Given the times and their gross amputations, I count myself blessed beyond words, surrounded as I am by a staunch circle of friends, family, community. The root, in fact and metaphor, of all good in my life.

We embattled Jesuits of West 98th Street in New York, enter a fourth year—count them!—of litigation, barely surviving the monetary maelstrom that engulfs Manhattan. A greedy, litigious landlord would have us banished from the premises—sooner the better.

We shall overcome—perhaps. Meantime (these days, every day is a meantime), we stand together. Thank you!

Thank you, Stephen Kelly, S.J., prisoner of conscience rooted (!) in biblical faith. Proud we are to name you friend and mentor.

My brother Philip and his family point the right way, and walk it, in what Scripture calls "this crooked generation." So do brothers John, Jim, Jerry, their spouses and progeny. I learn from you something of a Scripture come alive. Thank you.

Colleen and Dan Kelly suffered a cruel loss on 9/11. Their voices and example grace these pages. Thank you.

Last, and hardly least, thank you, Jeremy Langford, editor par excellence. Get it right! Is your bristling dictum, as you scrutinized every jot and tittle of this effort, with acute eye and faultless taste.

# Preface

The worst, the unimaginable. The month, date, hour, 9/11/9:30 a.m., are seared in the common memory.

But wait; is it possible that even the worst could further worsen?

It is possible, it came to pass. Within short weeks, retaliation and revenge were in the air, and the bombers took off in the night. Target, Afghanistan.

Fortified with the approval of the Catholic bishops and a Congress feverish with bellicosity, the president launched a new form of war. New, and by no means new. Shortly, his war is drowned in clichè and contradiction; a "war against terror."

Thus in a notorious irony, the terror named war seeks out its mirror image, the terror named despair. Gorgon to Gorgon, face to face.

Could there be found another way than the headlong rush to reprisal? Appalled, I opened the Scripture and came on a poetry of grief, forged in the fires of disaster.

Tragedy evoked the verses. Under the hammer blows of an all but unpronounceable Babylonian tyrant, Nebuchadnezzar, the unimaginable befell. Jerusalem was besieged (the temple sacked, the indiscriminate killing and starvation and flight into exile), composed a series of Lamentations, the book at hand.

Here was a clue, another way. It was like a finger pointing, first to the text, then to ourselves.

The verses are hardly to be thought a nosegay of pieties. Nothing of these, but an ancient, uncontained threnody, a tearing of ashen garments, a dance of berserkers. At the start, the emotion is wild, distempered, steeped in rage, furious at God, who stands accused of abandoning His own to the savagery of goys.

Remarkably, nothing of blasphemy is shortened, forbidden, or cleansed from the text.

On those raw pages, I met—myself, ourselves. The poetry is a pure outcry, out of ancient Jerusalem, out of the World Trade Center less than a year past.

Self-knowledge, I reflected, has its price. In Lamentations (this is the merciless mercy that shines in the poetry) we are spared nothing; nothing of flailing curses and denunciations. Ourselves, under winds of catastrophe wildly veering, like weather vanes in a tornado.

✦   ✦   ✦

That was the first mercy, to encounter one's self, ourselves, in the mirror of the text. To be implicitly granted time and place, allowing us ever so gradually and painfully, to recover balance, to breathe again.

✦   ✦   ✦

The author raises a painful question, and courageously (and so helpfully) sets to answering it. Thus confession of sin becomes a large theme of Lamentations.

Why, why did the awful event befall us? Why was the Temple reduced to rubble, the city sacked, noncombatants murdered, survivors driven into exile?

The answer was shockingly blunt. Because we had sinned, the poet insisted. Because long since we had fallen to idolatries, to worship of money and weaponry and domination and betrayal.

Hold the mirror, dare to look! In massive falling away, we came to resemble the idolatrous nations surrounding us. One of them, ourselves. For this we had become "the unchosen."

✦   ✦   ✦

After 9/11, confession of sin quickly became neglected, indeed an unthinkable discipline.

The "Why?" of our losses was a forbidden question. We Americans, sinners? We, "asking for it"?

From the White house we heard nothing of this. The assault on financial and military centers had no conceivable connection with our behavior in the world, the way we are perceived in the lens of victims. No, 9/11 was an act of unprovoked, gratuitous evil.

So went the myth.

For a time, it held firm.

✦   ✦   ✦

And what of the Church, what response to the war?

Not a word of contradiction or rebuke. Let the inflexible dogma of the innocents (ourselves), grossly wounded by the guilty (your president knows who)—let this stand unchallenged.

And from the bishops, worse, and less; not a single reference to the gospel.

Church and state, it shortly became clear, stood foursquare, in close collusion. A crusade! The bishops, demoralized by scandal, evangelically illiterate, walked *peri passu* with the warmaking state.

A warmaking Church, an oxymoron?

The twin towers fell to rubble. The twin powers turned to war.

Confession of guilt, the first gift of Lamentations. And the text offered a further mercy.

In ancient Jerusalem, a lightning bolt fell on the impregnable city, walled about by divine favor.

In Lamentations, fury against God and the enemy erupted. At times "God" and "enemy" powerfully merged. Indeed, as the unthinkable came to pass, God (as Isaiah reported) changed allegiance. God became the primordial, primary enemy of the "chosen."

Eventually the fury of the rejected subsided, yielding to confession of guilt. And finally, there came a healing submission, as a new mind and heart were born.

Let us submit to this awful decree. Let us mend our ways, in exile and shame coming on a saving wisdom. For even in Jerusalem, we were alienated from God and one another.

Let us yield before this awful decree, mend our ways, even in exile come on a saving wisdom.

We have served other gods, "the works of our hands," the "silver and chariots," greed, violence, idols, and icons of a deadly culture.

Turn, turn, turn.

After 9/11, did our Catholic community confess, repent sins of silence and complicity, greed and violence, homophobia, contempt toward women, racism, war-ism? Did we, through our bishops, speak a word of rebuke to the warmaking state?

Quite the opposite. The bishops' document stuttered and plodded along. Political and military decisions were approved, with a (harmless) caveat, weightless in the context of the indiscriminate weaponry at hand and the will to launch it.

Who among the authorities were listening anyway, who gave a damn for noncombatants, refugees, women and children, the aged—wherever these might dwell in ruined Afghanistan?

The sponsors of war closely resemble the weapons they create. And smart bombs, depleted uranium, land mines, rockets and tanks, rather than protecting "widows, and orphans, and strangers at the gate," are designed precisely to create "widows and orphans," to transform "strangers" into enemies, and enemies into corpses.

✦   ✦   ✦

Once again, war preempted the healing of humans, a gift celebrated in Lamentations.

War has shown the response of the warmaking state, toward its own citizens. A matter of utmost contempt. A rush to judgment would turn our tears to fiery steel, thrust weapons in our hands, and sow vengeance in our hearts.

Dramatized in the text is a far different process, a slow, painful walk toward holiness and enlarged humanity.

Bush's war has brutally dismembered the message of the book. The part is seized for the whole, anger and reprisal re-embraced as the only good.

Thus Lamentations is cast aside by a culture, voracious and stuck in place.

✦   ✦   ✦

We who mourn and resist (the two are close companions in Lamentations and the prophets) may see in the official contempt a notable irony.

Our book is dangerous and must be officially suppressed. It is dangerous, on this score. If the text were taken seriously, the war could not proceed.

Believers, take it seriously!

Lamentations is crucial, precious, a handbook of survival, and more.

Ponder it, welcome the pain of it, walk with it.

It lifts the flagging spirit, it enables a sturdy NO!

AFTER

When the towers fell
a conundrum;

Shall these from eternity
inherit the earth,
all debts amortized?

Gravity was ungracious,
a lateral blow
abetted, made an end.
They fell like Lucifer,

star of morning, our star
attraction, our access.

Nonetheless, a conundrum;
did God approve, did they prosper us?

The towers fell, money
amortized in pockets
emptied, once for all.

Why did they fall, what law
violated? Did Mammon
mortise the money
that raised them high, Mammon
anchoring the towers in cloud,
highbrow neighbors
of gated heaven and God?

"Fallen, fallen is Babylon the great . . .
they see the smoke
arise as she burns . . ."

We made pilgrimage there.
Confusion of tongues.

Some cried vengeance.
Others paced slow, pondering

—this or that of humans
drawn forth, dismembered.

a last day; Babylon
Remembered.

# Introduction

The year begins with war.
Our bombs fall day and night,
Hour after hour, by death
Abroad appeasing wrath,
Folly, and greed at home.
Upon our giddy tower
We'd oversway the world.
Our hate comes down to kill
Those whom we do not see,
For we have given up
Our sight to those in power
And to machines, and now
Are blind to all the world . . . .

(Wendell Berry, *A Timbered Choir: The Sabbath Poems 1979–1997.*
Washington, D.C.: Counterpoint Press, p. 125)

✦　✦　✦

*Lamentations*—the word speaks for itself. Something terrible, something literally beyond imagining, has befallen Jerusalem and its people.

"Befallen." Exactly. The skies have fallen. A proud clan, a proud city, lies in the dust. The Temple is gutted, the walls of the holy city a rubble. Prophecy is stilled, at least for a time—a time that seems an eternity. The elders and priests, those proud links of tradition and sacrifice and psalm—they are vanished from the scene, driven like cattle into slavery and exile.

National identity, or more exactly, imperial identity, is shattered.

It rested on unsteady piers, as was evident after the fact—militarism, a rigid class system of the prosperous and the deprived, worship emptied of concern for "the widow and orphan and stranger at the gate."

And perhaps most damaging of all, a naive assumption, common among the elite, that come what may, come war and greed and cruelties against the victimized—God was "on our side."

The conviction was simply taken for granted—irrefragable.

And why not? The Temple was a world wonder, the sacrifices spectacular in their scope and artistry, song and dance and solemn proclamation of the law. World trade flourished, coffers of palace and Temple were full.

The sky was the limit, literally. All signs pointed to divine approval.

1

But wait. God had news for the empire. On the horizon, a storm was gathering—its name was Babylon.

✦ ✦ ✦

It bore a truer name, a more awful one—divine fury. Jeremiah, his voice lost on the winds, was relentless, not to be silenced. The Temple was a coven of idolaters. Let priests and people vaunt, one day they would cower—the deity was outraged.

The words of the prophet served him, and the city, precisely nothing. The authorities cast over him the pelt of a scapegoat. He was a weaver of dire fantasies, in effect a turncoat against his own. He must be dealt with.

First he was ostracized, his writings publicly burned by the king. Then, cast in a dry well, he narrowly escaped death.

Nonetheless, his oracles were on the mark, cruelly, surgically so. Retribution lurked, disaster swiftly descended, as Lamentations attests.

✦ ✦ ✦

Given time, the book became a liturgical text, a yearly reminder of sin, grief, chastisement, and restoration.

God's love had taken an unutterably cruel form. But that love would weather the storm. Jerusalem would rise again, the exiles would return, rebuild the Temple and city walls. The faith of the remnant shone anew, chastised and purified.

✦ ✦ ✦

Lamentations also cast a long shadow forward in time. It became a precious midrash of Christian sensibility. On Good Friday, the service of *tenebrae* resounded in churches and chapels. Lights were extinguished, as evening came on. In the sanctuary a mounted triangle held a series of dark beeswax candles alight, topped by a single white taper, the light of Christ.

As each verse of Lamentations was announced, the grieving resounded in the dusk. A lighted candle was snuffed. Finally, only the topmost candle remained. Then it too was removed from place and hidden behind the altar, where it glowed mysteriously, as though in a closed tomb—Christ had died.

Now darkness enveloped the Church and world.

But that was not the final act. In a sublime, fragile gesture of hope, the candle was brought forth and restored in place, an augury of a further, unimaginable Event. Death was denied the last word.

In silence, the worshippers departed.

The symbolism, the threnody, the stripped altar and empty tabernacle, its door swung wide as though in final desolation—these formed an immensely moving mime. Lamentation indeed.

Unknown authors, singers, poets, survivors, strung together our hoop of songs. The sequence strikes one as both contrived and inspired, with the opening word of each strophe a letter of the Hebrew alphabet, from first to last.

The device lent discipline and continuity; wild grief was contained, grew bearable.

It is as though the exiles were also prisoners (which they were), chanting their grief through the bars of a prison or stockade.

Layer upon layer, contrasts and likenesses contend in the verses; despair, hope, resolve, bewilderment, anger, appeasement. The losses were unbearable; no, somehow they could be borne. Was not God still God—though God had turned about and spurned God's own?

Why, why, why this disaster? The text poses the tormenting question and more—it ventures an answer.

Thus, sin, our sin, has shaken the pillars of empire. What has befallen, we have brought upon ourselves. The moral universe stands vindicated. This is the word that comes through the text, dense, clogged with grief and loss. Despite all, a word of truth. And the bare bones of hope as well.

Why, why the awful events that befell the United States in late summer of 2001?

For this cause. An awesome "yang" has followed on a repeated, unrepented "yin." What has befallen us at the twin towers and the Pentagon—repeatedly and in more grievous measure, we have inflicted on others.

Daring to ask "why." Daring an answer, wounding as it may be to pride and ethos and national myths. Letting a harsh, wounding truth strike home.

Thus the saving themes of Lamentations: remorse, repentance, hope of reconciling.

Shall the like become possible to us, a people reeling and wounded?

## THE QUESTION

If the world's temperate zone,
then too
its cruel weather,
punishing, torrid, arctic.

If freedom, then two wills conflicting: wild Cain,
smooth-phrased Abel, too good
for foul actual life.

If shelter for sad shepherds,
then the wild verge of the heart,
extravagance, violence, the lamb
murdered, rot and stench.

If the way—
no way at all; way lost,
last chance, a potter's waste.

If fiery vine, sour lees at heart.

If silence, forbearance
under all malice—

O when
will You have done
imagining?

(DB)

## chapter one

# "Lonely, widowed, city of slaves . . ."
# (1:1–18)

**1:1–2** We are plunged without prelude into a scene of woe. The "bride of God" is widowed. Grief sits on every face; life is stricken to heart. No more pretense, no vaunting or show of power; days of wine and rose are vanished on the winds of war.

Drink the bitter cup to its lees.

✦ ✦ ✦

The American vintage of wrath was grown, harvested, and mixed— elsewhere, by other hands. From the opening verse, more than the autumn disaster in New York is at stake.

Our sin is that of the Jerusalem of Jeremiah: idolatry. The World Trade Center (the name implies the sin) together with the Pentagon, are quite literally places of worship. There, world domination, monetary and military, is cozened, calculated, paid tribute.

Such worship has exacted a horrendous price, for generations. And always (until a day now seared in memory), the price was paid by others than us.

Thus the lamentation, rightly taken, falls from the stricken lips of the victimized, the invaded and sanctioned and bombed peoples who fall (too bad for them!) afoul of the American hegemony.

Only tardily, only a comparatively few Americans claim the threnody, take it to heart and lips. From those at the highest level of authority, from media and military, arises a clamorous outcry for vengeance and retaliation.

Confession of sin, questioning of behavior, submitting to chastisement— these are emotions foreign to the national soul, a lost language of Ur.

✦ ✦ ✦

In the lament, we read of malice and the seeking of vengeance. But this is a background clamor. The major theme is other: lingering grief, confession of sin, purpose of amendment.

It is the word of God, instructive, meant for our lips, our chastening and healing.

The symbols are of prebirth and postpartum, both:

> How  lonely she is now,
> the once crowded city!
>
> Widowed is she,
> who was mistress over nations;
>
> The princess among the provinces
> have been made toiling slaves. (1:1)

In magical New York—the cynosure of the eyes of the nation, the self-proclaimed "capital of the world" —mighty towers were toppled.

Let it be confessed, the first, indispensable, humiliating admission. The ruin we have wantonly sown abroad has turned about and struck home.

✦   ✦   ✦

"How lonely . . ." We Americans are more and more isolated on the world scene. The Bush administration has rejected the Kyoto agreement on global warming, has rejected an agreement to regulate the trade of small arms, has distanced itself from the Antiballistic Missile Treaty, the Comprehensive Nuclear Test Ban Treaty, and the Biological Weapons Convention.

The U.S. has refused to ratify the proposed International Criminal Court of Justice. To nullify the effort, America is proposing something to be known as The American Service Members Protection Act. This will authorize military force to free any American soldier taken into International Criminal Court custody. Touch us not!

✦   ✦   ✦

After bombing eighteen countries in the last decades, after incursions and manipulations and lethal sanctions and the seizure of world markets and the reduction of multitudes to economic enslavement—after all this, the towers were struck, ejecting their human cargo like rubbish. And the Pentagon was breached.

To such horrendous effect, was there no cause attached?

All said, all done to insure "national security," to punish enemies—what an illusion! How vulnerable are the mighty, we the "mistress over nations."

✦  ✦  ✦

Bitterly she weeps at night,
tears upon her cheeks,

With not one to console her
of all her dear ones;

Her friends have all betrayed her
and become her enemies.  (1:2)

The scene is of utter desolation, a dark night of the spirit. The reigning images of an omnipotent warrior god have dissolved, fled the soul, the Temple, the grandiose cityscape.

Likewise overthrown is a pier of identity jealously set in place, guarded and exploited through the ages; we, "the chosen."

Brutally, against all tradition and expectation, the tribe is—unchosen.

Worse. In a crushing irony, Babylon the merciless claims the divine favor snatched from Jerusalem.

✦  ✦  ✦

Friends become enemies; those once trustworthy and near turn traitors. Whatever the reference, the grief lies deeper than grief; sanity and good sense are crushed out of recognition.

What sorer loss than that of trust between friends?

We humans flourish through trust and friendship—or we die for lack of these, social and personal realities, both. The web of life is woven close; survival demands fidelity to the design, hands and eyes carefully, skillfully weaving and repairing.

For we ourselves figure in the pattern, we weave and weave—or the threads fray and tangle, the pattern falls apart.

✦  ✦  ✦

**1:3**

Judah has fled into exile
from oppression and cruel slavery;

Yet where she lives among the nations,
she finds no place to rest.

All her persecutors come upon her
where she is narrowly confined.

Despite the rather clumsy translation, "exile" is clearly one with "oppression and cruel slavery." We are mourning in exile, a historical reality and a spiritual one as well, an ancient uprooting and "non-belonging"; and a modern one too—or a postmodern, which comes to much the same.

✦   ✦   ✦

This is the sensibility Paul commends to the believing community. "Be not conformed to this world," he warns.

The warning has never been more exactly to the point, the situation of Christians in America.

"Con-formity" with this world implies several metaphors: a kind of grafting on to worldly ethos, a nonargument with its ideologies and appetites, a falling in step with its projects.

Or a disappearing into its vortex. Drowning there, suffocating.

✦   ✦   ✦

As in the winter of 2001, Bush's war proceeds apace against the all-but-decimated, impoverished people of Afghanistan.

An immediate "statement" was issued by the Catholic bishops. The outmoded stipulations of the "just war theory" once more were hauled out. Mr. President, in effect, full speed ahead!

✦   ✦   ✦

And I thought, in a mood veering between dejection and recognition: déjà vu—with a difference.

Vietnam had endured fifteen years of American napalm and bombs. A number of us spoke up, wrote, marched, destroyed draft files, and went to prison. And the bishops were mum as a midnight graveyard.

In an ironic way, their silence was fitting. Quite literally, they had nothing to offer.

Year 2001, yet another war. And the bishops, not to be caught napping, issue "a statement."

They have nothing to offer—and they lack the grace to keep silent. They offer—nothing.

An old lesson, and a new. The bishops willy nilly are fulfilling the metaphors suggested by Paul. They are grafted onto the world, that "tree of the knowledge of good and evil," and its ambiguous fruits. They have no argument with the ethos of mass killing. They fall in step with a vile project, enlisting themselves (and us?) "for the duration."

And what of an echo of the gospel teaching, "Love your enemies?"

Astonishing, and weirdly instructive, the bishops' statement made no reference, even in passing, to the teaching and example of Christ.

Thus our verse is (not so subtly) altered, in denial of Christ and Paul, to something like:

> Where she lives among the nations,
> She finds a place to rest.

"A place to rest" indeed.

✦　✦　✦

The final strophe of verse 3 presents the normal ("normal," underscored) situation of the believing community. This is not lightly stated.

The "finding rest among the nations" is the abnormal, the weird. In truth, the betrayal.

Here a drama, cruel, exact—normal. JPS has it thus:

> All her persecutors overtook her
> in the narrow places.

Indicating as well, that the Hebrew is uncertain. NAB has roughly the same idea:

> All her persecutors come upon her
> where she is narrowly confined.

In either version, one notes a constriction, as though of prisoners held in a kind of holding tank.

A war is declared, believers resist. Speedily they are under duress, convicted of serious charges, imprisoned.

The one follows the other, war, then prison—as night the day.

In sum, for years my friends, my brother and I have resisted the cause that the bishops support.

With the integrity of the gospel in question (one almost thought, in jeopardy), let us ponder: who is leading whom, who is misleading?

✦　✦　✦

**1:4**

> The roads to Zion mourn,
> for lack of pilgrims going to her feasts;
> All her gateways are deserted,
> her priests groan,

Her virgins sigh,
she is in bitter grief.

Nature takes up the plaint. The rhythms of worship, the great days that awakened remembrance, rejoicing, confidence in the saving acts of God, those acts of renewal and healing and return—no more.

The stones of the road find voice: "no more, no more . . ."

Could it be imagined that catastrophes of war, bombings, massed forces moving against the innocent, misery and displacement and death—that these leave worship untouched, neutral?

Or that—a worse case by far—if the priests react to the moral disaster with silence or a "statement" of approval—shall that worship speak for the God of peace, for Jesus, capitally condemned by the empire?

Another task is called for. Let priests who are faithful to the gospel speak up, let them resist the infamy of state and church marching to a war drum. Let them "groan."

✦   ✦   ✦

And those "virgins," who are they?

They are the innocents under fire, the children and the aged, the refugees, evicted, starving, freezing, the "collateral damage" of technological savagery.

As the bombers punish the innocent and destroy the ecology, we think of those who flee the snare and fall into the trap.

For the impoverished of Afghanistan, the choices are narrow as a gimlet; death from the air, death by starvation.

✦   ✦   ✦

Another sense of "virgins" is dear to the Bible—those whose hearts are untrammeled, who are unswayed by the nonsense of "just war" confabulations. The death by violence of one child, as they know, puts the theory to naught.

These are the "pure of heart" blessed by Jesus, the "unconformed to this world" commended by Paul. The fevers and chills, the flags and slogans pass them by.

Hardly audible amid the chaos and clamor, they plead for the victims. This is their offering, sorry and ineffectual as it must be accounted.

Nonetheless, their reward is sure: they shall "see God," the God of peace.

✦   ✦   ✦

**1:5**

> Her foes are uppermost,
> her enemies are at ease;
>
> God has punished her
> for her many sins.
>
> Her little ones have gone away,
> captive before the foe.

Like an upper and lower millstone, strophes 1 and 3 grind strophe 2 close and hard. It is as though from wheat, flour were being painfully ground.

Terrifying. From millstone to oven, bread of truth is in the making.

And yet, and yet. One thinks: best keep God out of the night-ridden images. Better a philosophic finger, pointing. The nature of the universe is such, and stands firm: "what goes around, comes around."

Let it be said plain. God does not grant victory, God does not decree defeat. The gods of the victorious grant victory; the same gods decree defeat.

In wartime, gods of war take command. The combatants regress to a morality of dog eat dog. They cast aside saving, sane images and resources and instructors—Christ, gospel, sanity itself.

If the American bishops were consistent and honorable, they would publicly burn the Gospels. Then they would contrive a liturgy of a different sort, forming a procession, entering a church, holding aloft *The Marine Handbook of War*. The antigospel would be placed on the high altar and incensed.

✦ ✦ ✦

**1:6–7**

> Gone from daughter Zion
> is all her glory;
>
> Her princes like rams
> that find no pasture,
>
> Have gone off without strength
> before their captors.

Striking throughout the threnody are feminine images. Also, social realities are rendered intensely personal. The city is "daughter" of the mourners; they conversely, see themselves as her mother.

Jerusalem is a conglomerate of high culture to be sure, gleaming with palace and temple and elegant mansions. Then the contrasts and contradictions as well: slovenly quarters of forced laborers, military barracks, centers of commerce and trade, houses of prostitution, prisons . . .

Ah, but beloved Zion is more than these! It is "glory," here summoned by the text, a glory all the more precious and radiant for being brutally quenched, a memory, a fantasy.

Glory. It is (no, alas it was)—feminine soul, peerless beauty, a heartbeat, dance, song, memories, gardens, prophets, incense, and altar.

Also grand events and memories: the quest for justice and the falling short, exodus from Egypt, manna in the desert, water flowing from sere rock, divine fury, and forgiveness—the indefinable treasures amassed through centuries of grief and glory.

Sound the passing bell—gone, gone!

✦　✦　✦

Jerusalem is mindful of the days
of her wretched homelessness,

When her people fell into enemy hands,
and she had no one to help her,

When her foes gloated over her,
laughed at her ruin.

Memories do not rebuild walls, nor restore a people destroyed. Generations passed, the exile went on, brutish, unending.

In the present, in the eyes of the conquerors, this is a "former" nation, Zion, its memories fictive and fading.

Of what point this dwelling on the past? It is lost, done with. To those born in Babylon, as to those born in the wilderness after Egypt, memories count for less and less. They are old wives' tales, wisps of fog dispersed by every sunrise.

✦　✦　✦

Still, a contrary current gains voice in the verses. It can never be entirely stifled. Let us not allow the memories to die—memories of the great ancestors, their teaching and worship, the year's rhythms, kosher discipline, daily prayer. Even in despair, turn toward Jerusalem!

Memory is a bitter herb: "foes . . . gloating . . . homelessness . . . ruin";

sharp on the tongue, in the mind, memory heals, it confers the will to endure.

✦ ✦ ✦

**1:8–11**

> Through the sin of which she is guilty,
> Jerusalem is defiled.
>
> All who esteemed her, think her vile
> now that they see her nakedness.
>
> She herself groans
> and turns away.

The image of harlotry haunts the prophets, and the God of the prophets as well (cc Jeremiah 2, 3, and passim). Here the image is resumed, with passion—almost, one thinks, with a vengeance.

The image is precise, merciless. Naked the beloved stands, shamed, viewed with scorn. The truth is out. All mark it, she is stripped to near nothing.

Still, the shameful scene is also redemptive. To herself as well, the truth is out.

Then yield before it, a truth long neglected and ignored. You stand guilty of idolatry, of breach of covenant. You have bowed before gods of power, riches, pride of place, violence.

✦ ✦ ✦

> Arrogant, indifferent, contemptuous of international law, both dismissive and manipulative of the United Nations—this (the U.S.) is now the most dangerous power the world has ever known—the authentic "rogue state"— but a rogue state of colossal military and economic might.
>
> And Europe, especially the United Kingdom, is both compliant and complicit; or as Cassius in "Julius Caesar" put it, we "peep about to find ourselves dishonorable graves." (Harold Pinter; address at the University of Florence; nb, 9/10/01)

✦ ✦ ✦

In Lamentations, the Christian default also stands revealed. American religion, in the purview of American empire, provokes no quarrel, no questioning. Instead of uttering a prophetic outcry, the leaders fall in line. By compliant silence and complicit word, the Church shows herself reliable, a collaborator—the god is on our side.

✦ ✦ ✦

But here is a word that goes counter. The truth is out. She is naked, and shamed.

> Her filth is on her skirt;
> she gave no thought how she would end.
>
> Astounding is her downfall,
> with no one to console her.
>
> Look, O God upon her misery,
> for the enemy has triumphed! (1:9)

Filth on her skirt. A shocking, unseemly image, at first glance.

Glance again, context is everything. The filth is idolatry; it stains garment and soul. It is cleansed only by conversion of heart.

And fealty to idols brings worse: the worshippers fall to amnesia. Serving the gods, we forget—the neighbor, the works of compassion and justice.

✦ ✦ ✦

In the first prayer of Lamentations, two versions offer a contrast worth noting.

Our NAB: "Look upon her misery." JPS: "see . . . my misery."

Thus the mourner, praying for another (others), is transformed. Now it is fallen Jerusalem, rather than a bystander or witness of the catastrophe, who raises a prayer.

If the second version is reliable (and it indisputably is), we have quite a moment.

In former verses, suffering Jerusalem conveyed her plight in descriptive tropes. Now she ventures a petition of direct address.

And even more striking, as noted, the sufferer herself prays. She begs a remission of woe.

✦ ✦ ✦

"The enemy" alas, the one who wrought her ruin, is omnipresent to her mind. No transformation; a word (even a word of prayer!), and the foe is frozen in time and place. Babylon, fifth century. Enemy.

We shall hear again of this anger and unforgiveness—as immediately follows:

The foe stretched out his hand
to all her treasures;

She has seen those nations
enter her sanctuary

Whom You forbade to come
into Your assembly. (1:10)

That foe again. Self declared or so designated (or both), the enemy
abides in the text, underscored, ineradicable.

And God, by every implication, has allowed the catastrophe, if not
approved it.

The "treasures" can be understood in a double sense. The first is obvi-
ous. The books of Daniel (chapter 5) and Jeremiah (chapter 52) tell of the
treasures of the Temple, vessels and furnishings, stripped and carried off
to enrich the shrines of the Babylonians.

Other, less palpable "treasures" are also mourned. Daniel and his companions are poignant witnesses of the loss: liturgy and the law, memories
of the deeds of God summoned throughout the liturgical year, sacrifice
and sin offerings, the blessings implied in discipline of kosher.

✦   ✦   ✦

The presence of goys in the sanctuary must be accounted a blasphemy.
For the invaders arrive accompanied by their gods.

And worse is yet to come, as Daniel records. In December of 167 CE,
the "abomination of desolation" was set up in the Temple of Jerusalem by
the Greek ruler Antiochus.

✦   ✦   ✦

We Christians too must mourn the presence of alien deities in our sanctuaries.

A war is underway. Flags, ordinarily kept more or less discreetly in the
background, are placed prominently in sanctuaries. "For the duration"
the national gods stand there, challenging the Gospel of peace.

And the words of Lamentations are fulfilled; idols reign, they seize the
treasures of the faithful, the Word, the Bread and Cup.

The flag implies bloodshed, "just wars," enmities, the Church aping
the behavior of the state. The flag countenances deceit, betrayal, untruth,
demonizing, "collateral damage" (which is to say, murder of the innocent), the ecology violated.

What of the Eucharist, symbol of reconciliation and nonviolence? What can those words mean now, "My Body, given for you," "the cup of My Blood, poured out for you"?

What of Christ's command to love our enemies, what of the crucified One of Calvary?

✦ ✦ ✦

War sets the clocks, the true and awful hour. The nation is at war; so is the Church. The flag, not the gospel, announces time, mood, apt response.

It bears repeating. The nation is at war. So is the Church.

"For the duration," though the gospel calls believers to rebuke and resist a murderous national mood, the Bible is a closed book. Closed by ecclesiastical hands.

✦ ✦ ✦

We will know hunger and thirst, in more senses than one—in more senses say, than the hunger and thirst of refugees, fleeing in the frigid mountains of Afghanistan.

> All her people groan,
> searching for bread;
>
> They give their treasures for food,
> to retain the breath of life.
>
> "Look O God, and see
> how worthless I have become!" (1:11)

Bread again, and the bare bones of survival. Implied as well, the bare bones of truth: bones broken, scattered like kindling wood, the bread of truth tossed to the dogs of war.

✦ ✦ ✦

And a long, personal, impassioned plea is underway. For awhile ("for the duration" ?), no mere description of the impasse will do.

Instead, a daring, lyric leap; judgment is reversed. God must be summoned vis-à-vis:

> "Look O God and see,
> how worthless I have become!"

Exactly—worthless, the price tag tied to the flesh of the living. Multitudes, in the estimate of Mars, are better dead; or they soon will be dead. Without worth in any case, living or dead.

It is wartime. Humans are expendable. So is the human itself, a sense of one's own humanity, of the foe's.

Human life, cheap if not worthless.

✦  ✦  ✦

## 1:12

Come, all you who pass by the way,
look and see

Whether there is any suffering
like my suffering,

Which was dealt me
when God afflicted me
on the day of blazing wrath.

✦  ✦  ✦

In the first few days after the destruction of the World Trade Center, as we strive to understand, as we continue to work, search for hope and pray, we also ask again and again for forgiveness. Please forgive us, as our civilizations continue to unfold their long histories of violence.

Forgive us our anger, hate and drive for retribution. Forgive us our confusion and failure. We pray for the grace to maintain our faith and live out our pacifist convictions. We ask forgiveness for our sins. (*Catholic Worker*, October 2001)

✦  ✦  ✦

Our text is a long susurration of grief and agony.

There are those who suffer greatly: exiles, refugees, slaves, bare survivors. They are given voice here, the voiceless, the wretched of the earth.

Thus the Bible, its God, its prophets and witnesses speak for those pushed to the verge of the world, those who live and die anonymous, unsung, statistics in the ledgers of the Olympians. Thus the ironbound decree.

But God is not mocked, the God of "widows and orphans and strangers at the gate." In these pages, the victims have voice.

All honor to the witnesses, who rebut and rebuke the mighty.

✦  ✦  ✦

**1:13**

> From on high God sent fire
> down, into my very frame,
>
> Spread a net for my feet
> and overthrew me,
>
> left me desolate,
> in pain all the day.

The "I," "me," stand surrogate for the holy city as it suffers destruction, its people decimated under a brutal triage, the survivors exiled.

All are given voice, as though the lament issued from a Greek chorus. God "sent fire," God "spread a net." The images propel the action forward, even as they interpret it.

✦ ✦ ✦

Let it be confessed, for a long time kings and people admitted nothing of guilt.

The moral universe, ineluctable, retributive, was also patient, and awaited its moment.

Ezekiel saw the atrocious decline and fall of temple religion (chapter 8). He tells of the idolatries practiced in secret corners of the Temple, infecting priests and worshippers, women and men, alike.

Then from afar sounded a drumbeat of doom—the Babylonian forces gathering under Sennacherib. "Fire, net" indeed.

More—"God . . . fire and net." Faith impels the attribution, a faith worthy of Job.

Through faith the images make a kind of dark sense—the burning, the entanglement, how awful and apt.

✦ ✦ ✦

**1:15–16**

> All the mighty ones in my midst
> God has cast away;
>
> God summoned an army against me
> to crush my young men;
>
> God has trodden in the wine press
> virgin daughter Juda.

✦ ✦ ✦

Rumor of war, then war. What a dreary, immemorial clichè the text evokes!

The great ones are "cast away." Does the text not invite us to summon the ancestors to judgment? The kings of Israel, Saul, David, Solomon, Hezekiah, and the others—they lived unfaithful and unfree, waged wars of extermination, betrayed friend and foe, looted, scorched the earth. They were merciless, contemptuous of the victims whom they and their wars created, then cast away.

✦ ✦ ✦

Those who declare war, delegate others to the dirty work.

And what of the instigators, those who set the chariots in motion and flog the war horses? Old and honored, or old and dishonored (here, interestingly, they are "cast away" )—they die in their beds. It is the "young men" who, among others, must pay up and die. War is a wine press. In an extended, scorching image, God, strangely divided in mind, announces to Isaiah that the day of "vengeance" is also the day of "redeeming."

✦ ✦ ✦

Another anomaly of the Isaian text. In Christian piety,

> One
> treads the wine press
> alone,
>
> and
> of My people
>
> there was
> no one
>
> with
> Me . . . (63:3)

That One is identified as Jesus lamenting, as He undergoes His passion.

But the context hardly bears out the image of vulnerable submission. Far from it. Indeed the text is a war cry, steeped in blood and wrath:

> I trod them in my anger
> and trampled them down
> in my wrath.

> Their blood spurted
> on my garments,
> all my apparel I stained. (63:3)

A strange solitary campaign, and a reproof as well. Where is that multitude of the chosen, warriors all? Why do they not advance with the god, to decimate the hated Edomites?

Alas, on his own, in an appalling bloodletting, the deity disposes of the enemy.

Solitary, as is apparent, but hardly suffering.

> So my own arm
> brought about the victory,
>
> and my own wrath
> lent me its support.
>
> In my anger
> I trampled down
> the peoples,
>
> I crushed them
> in my wrath.
>
> And I let their blood
> run out
> upon the ground. (63:5–6)

✦ ✦ ✦

No merely human commander this, but a superhuman berserker!

No swords into plowshares here—the image is sanguinary, recessive. It is drawn from the heady days of empire; the god of Saul, David, and Solomon, ravages the earth.

✦ ✦ ✦

**1:17–18**

> Zion stretched out her hands,
> but there was no one to console her.
>
> God gave orders against Jacob
> for his neighbors to be his foes;
>
> Jerusalem has become in their midst
> a thing unclean.

The scene: a woman's hands are extended. She is a suppliant in a male world.

The world is hardly to be thought her world, responding to her need and that of her children, practiced in tenderness. Nothing of this. Too bad for her—she must make do or not, in a world of warriors.

For centuries during the era of the kings, feminine images were rare indeed. Only now and again, through the prophets, is a woman heard from, or her God.

Now, in defeat she "stretches out her hands." In the days of glory, hands had other uses. They were invariably male, they brandished a sword.

Males seldom yielded before the supplications of women.

Now, "she" must endure a like heartlessness—no mercy. It is as though her cry served only to aggravate bloodlust. The response is lethal, heartless.

The Revolutionary Association of the Women of Afghanistan (RAWA) wrote that "the fundamentalist terrorists [the Tailban] would devour their creators."

Let Americans be warned, wrote the women.

Their prediction was appallingly verified in the summer of 2001.

After the tragedy, the Afghan women sent a message of condolence. Its words were remarkable, one thinks, for psychological acuity:

> We send words of deep sorrow and solidarity with the American people. We believe however, that attacking Afghanistan and killing its most ruined and destitute people, will not in any way decrease the grief of the American people.

Previously, RAWA had written:

> The most treacherous, most criminal, most anti-democracy and anti-women fundamentalists . . . the Taliban, have committed every possible heinous crime against our people. They would feel no shame in committing such crimes against the American people . . . in order to gain and maintain their power . . .

✦  ✦  ✦

The deity of our text turns and turns about. The chosen are unchosen, goy warriors are made instruments of judgment, "neighbors" turn to "foes."

This is history, writ plain, the assault of the Assyrians against Jerusalem. The proud city fell.

To be sure, ours is a God who delights in harsh ironies. Thus, the Assyrian commander of "a great army" . . . , at the conduit of the upper pool speaks to the leaders of Jerusalem:

> Was it without God's will that I have come up to destroy this land?
> God said to me, "Go up and destroy that land"
> (Isaiah 36:10)

✦   ✦   ✦

Jerusalem, dust and ashes. And after the fact, the fall, a moral judgment intrudes—the city was "a thing unclean." It was true all along, and ignored.

Ezekiel was led on a guided tour of the Temple. He saw a catalog of horrors, culminating in this:

> Then he brought me into the inner court of God's house, and there at the door of God's temple, between the vestibule and the altar, were about twenty-five men with their backs to God's temple and their faces toward the east. They were bowing down to the sun.
> "Do you see, son of man?" he asked me. "Is it such a trivial matter for the house of Juda that they do the abominable things they have done here—for they have filled the land with violence and again and again they have provoked me—that now they must put the branch to My nose?
> "Therefore I in turn will act furiously. I will not look upon them with pity nor will I show mercy." (chapter 8)

✦   ✦   ✦

"Put the branch to My nose . . ."

> A reference perhaps to the Egyptian sun god Re, pictured with a vine branch at his nose, signifying the transfer of creative power (divine breath) to living things. (NAM)

✦  ✦  ✦

Thus the following, v. 18: judgment against herself, and self-proclaimed:

> God is just;
> I have defied His command.
>
> Listen, all you peoples,
> and behold my suffering;
>
> My maidens and my youths
> have gone into captivity.

The truth includes in its orbit more than the delinquent. How could it not? As she mourns, her gaze turns abroad.

She is a sorry illustration of a universal truth. "Listen" then, and be warned. Disobedience, defection from the God of life in favor of the gods, brings unutterable havoc.

Isaiah had seen it, idolatry in full panoply:

> their land is full of silver and gold,
> and there is no end to their treasures;
>
> Their land is filled with horses
> and there is no end to their chariots;
>
> Their land is full of idols;
> they worship the works of their hands . . . (2:6–8)

✦  ✦  ✦

"Their," be it noted, and "they." Not "our" and "we." The radical disowning of his people by a proud, self-conscious mind. Isaiah judges, he is not included in the judgment.  It is "they" who pay fealty to idols, "silver" and "chariots," greed and violence.

Be they far from me, Isaiah. Be You near to me, true God.

A devastating social critique.

And hardly waiting on disaster, but before the fact, the breaching of the walls, the killing and enslavement. Before all this, and in the teeth of prosperity, the prophesy: doom.

## chapter two

# "O, give heed to my groaning" (1:19–2:17)

**1:19**

> I cried out to my lovers,
> but they failed me.
>
> My priests and my elders
> perished in the city;
>
> when they sought food for themselves,
> they found it not.

✦ ✦ ✦

The first loss is a failure of love, or perhaps of friendship. The text is ambiguous—is the failure in fact a betrayal? (JPS would have it so: "My friends . . . played me false").

And what affection! We hold in hand, scattered in the poetry like seeds of wildflowers from Hades, a litany of loss: "her dear ones . . . her friends . . . her priests . . . her virgins . . . her little ones . . . her princes . . . her people . . . my young men . . . my sons . . . my maidens and my youths . . ."

Alas, the garden is torn up, the flowers trampled.

The ornaments of high civilization, the noblest and bravest, the elite of family and attainment—these are destroyed. They died in the holy city, or on the road to exile, or in unendurable slavery.

✦ ✦ ✦

In our verse, the "my," repeatedly mourning both priests and elders, heightens the loss. It is irreparable, beyond consoling. They, they were mine, heart of my heart. They are gone.

And the grief is heightened by the scene of their death; many perished in the city they adorned. Priestly worship was the jewel of the Temple foil, wisdom of the elders graced the populace.

Lament indeed. Irreplaceable lives, a tradition of prophecy and torah, feasts of renewal and recalling—gone. Or so in a bitter time, it seemed.

✦   ✦   ✦

Verses 20–22 turn from anguished description of the common plight, to equally anguished prayer:

> Look, O God, on my distress;
> all within me is in ferment,
>
> My heart recoils within me
> from my monstrous rebellion.
>
> In the streets the sword bereaves,
> at home death stalks.

Faced with words of an anguish beyond bearing, the poet is all but reduced to silence.

And a Catholic worker, imprisoned for a conscientious action against war, writes from prison of the awful event of summer 2001:

> In death, something is broken and cannot be repaired; there is a woundedness that refuses to be healed, a pain that disdains comfort. Perhaps what is needed is not talk and action, but silence and reflection.
>
> A national day or week or month of silence. No television, no radio, no mumbling ministers, just silence and prayer and presence to this terrible reality of death and suffering. Perhaps in prayer and silence and powerlessness, God can enter our wounds and suffering and as with Lazarus, bring new life out of death. (Jeff Dietrich, (Los Angeles) *Catholic Radical,* winter 2001)

✦   ✦   ✦

"My monstrous rebellion." A harsh judgment—the more remarkably, it is lodged against herself, her people.

The vast panoply of David and Solomon lies in rubble. The army, the treasury, the Temple and palace bespeak only grief and loss. And through travail, the people of Jerusalem are transformed.

This is the first wonder, the primary mercy. The city is disfigured, beset. And the threnody renounces images of power and glory—and most enticing of all, the sword.

Sensibility has undergone a sea change. The voice that speaks for all is no longer a warrior's or a proud ruler's. It is the lorn voice of a woman.

✦  ✦  ✦

The second change is no less remarkable. At long last, she has come to the truth of her condition before God. No need for the deity to shake the heavens with fury, to launch thunderbolts against her default. She knows, she judges: "my monstrous rebellion." Or another version: "How wrong I was to disobey" (JPS).

"Rebellion . . . wrong"—need the contrast be spelled out? In the days of the empire, no king or warrior or priest spoke in such terms, no one knew— or so much as cared to know. Much less to renounce.

Now, on her knees, she knows what the prophets knew: sin, compounded in the social, military, economic, yes the religious systems. Sin pursuing enemies, sin coming down hard on the defenseless.

She speaks as the prophets spoke.

✦  ✦  ✦

But such wisdom arises only in somber retrospect. Whipped, defeated, on the road to exile, like the wife of Lot she turns for a last look of love and love lost. The smoke, the rubble, the stench.

A monstrous rebellion indeed. Had not her idolatries worked an unthinkable act, forcing God to abandon the Temple and flee into exile? Ezekiel is the witness:

> "Human one," God asked me,
> "do you see what they are doing?
>
> "do you see the great abominations
> that the house of Israel
> is practicing here,
>
> "so that I
> must depart
>
> "from
> My
> sanctuary? . . ."
>
> Then the glory of God
> left the threshold of the temple . . .
>
> The glory of God
> rose from the city,

and took a stand
on the mountain
which is
to the east

of
the
city. (8:6; 10:18; 11:23)

✦   ✦   ✦

In memory, the witness returns to Jerusalem. Her eyes, dimmed with tears, roam about the beloved city.

Ezekiel again is the witness. Abroad, death roams unchallenged, calculated death:

Then God said,
"Pass through Jerusalem,

mark an X on the foreheads of those who moan and groan

over the abominations
practiced within it."

To the others
I heard God say,

"Pass through the city . . .
and strike!

Do not
look on them
with pity,

nor show
any mercy! . . .

But do not touch
any

marked
with
X . . ." (9:4–6)

✦   ✦   ✦

In verse 21 of Lamentations the mourner is caught in a dilemma, of two minds. Whence came the catastrophe? Is it of God, is it of the Assyrians?

Give heed to my groaning;
there is no one to console me.

All my enemies rejoice at my misfortune;
it is You who has wrought it.

Bring on the day you have proclaimed,
that they may be even as I.

It is of both God and the Assyrians. But faith forbids that she call God
to accounts.

The same faith hardly forbids the summoning of vengeance. Quite the
contrary. Intensely the theme continues:

Let all their evil come before You; deal with them

as You have dealt with me
for all my sins;

My groans are many
and I am sick at heart. (1:22)

We have an equation strongly presumed. God, she confesses, is just.

May that justice vindicate itself—*quid pro quo*, equal treatment under
law. This: "An eye for an eye."

But a question intervenes like a raised, halting hand: Will destruction
of her enemies, in the name of God's justice—will this mitigate her own
sufferings? Or is there another way than vengeance, a better?

On this serious subject, Christians have a midrash of note. It takes the
form of a strong charge:

My command to you is;
love your enemies,

pray
for your persecutors.

Thus
you will show yourselves

sons and daughters
of

your
heavenly
Father . . . (Matthew 5:44–45)

✦   ✦   ✦

From a letter to the *Chicago Tribune*, 9/25/01:

My husband, Craig Amundson of the U.S. army, lost
his life at the Pentagon on Sept. 11 . . .

Losing my 28-year-old husband and father of our two
young children, is a terrible and painful experience . . .

I have heard angry rhetoric by some Americans, including many of our nation's leaders, who advise a heavy
dose of revenge and punishment.

To those leaders, I would like to make clear that my
family and I take no comfort in your words of rage . . .
Your words and immanent acts of revenge only amplify
our family's suffering, deny us the dignity of remember-
ing our loved one in a way that would have made him
proud, and mock his vision of America as a peacemaker
in the world community . . .

Craig would not have wanted a violent response to
avenge his death. And I cannot see how good can come
of it. Mohandas Gandhi said: "An eye for an eye only
makes the whole world blind" . . .

I call on our national leaders to find the courage to
respond to this incomprehensible tragedy by breaking the
cycle of violence . . . (Amber Amundson)

✦   ✦   ✦

**2:1**

God in wrath
has detested daughter Zion,

has cast down from heaven to earth
the glory of Israel,

Unmindful of God's footstool
on the day of wrath.

What a strange faith! Do we conclude that a totally unknown terrain,
little light is shed?
The faithful one wavers uneasily between the agents of her downfall.
Whom to blame, whom to indict? This one, no—that one . . .

For now, in this mood, let it be said as clearly as word and trope can convey: God has wrought this horror.

But no. This way and that, the mirror of conscience turns, darkness reflecting only the dark.

It was formerly and just as strongly stated—our sins have brought this horror:

> God has punished her
> for her many sins. (1:5)

And again:

> Through the sins of which she is guilty,
> Jerusalem is defiled. (1:8)

Yet again:

> God has kept watch
> over my sins. (1:14)

✦   ✦   ✦

"God . . . has detested daughter Zion." "A detested daughter"—could a perversion more offensive to nature be imagined?

To the father, a daughter is the very apple of his eye, a pride and joy. Even in a culture of male bonding, the affection (not, to be sure, the primogeniture and portion) abides strongly. But here?

The hardening of heart, the casting out, is awful, unbearable. It cannot be squared with logic, cannot be undone by summoning affectionate memories. It stands there, a text turned icy, a testimony; rejection, the beloved put to the door.

Summon a trope then—one that bespeaks a heart mortally wounded. Daughter, and detested. Mourn and mourn.

✦   ✦   ✦

Another image in this pharmacology of tears.

"Cast down from heaven to earth . . ."

How more strongly, poignantly—more wrongly stated! Wrongly? A suggestion, an authorial implication whispers in the text, the trope.

This, the mourner(s) stand, not with the beleaguered prophets of resistance (Isaiah, Jeremiah, Ezekiel, Daniel, and the others). Rather, she mourns for the downfall, first of the great Temple ("glory of Israel") and (the same probably), "footstool." And by implication, destruction of the imperial system of David and Solomon, economic, military, religious.

✦   ✦   ✦

A polluted "heaven," in sum. Heaven for a few; hell for the many. For nobles and priests and merchants, vast wealth. For the multitudes, the "widows and orphans and strangers at the gate," in plain denial of God's will, pervasive misery.

This for many; corvÈes under the lash were set to constructing an overbearing Temple and palace. The people groaned under the cost of endless wars.

✦   ✦   ✦

And of that "glory," that "footstool," we have heard much from Ezekiel and the other prophets—and little to its credit. In sum, an ideology has seized and absorbed a theology, an honored tradition. Israel comes more and more to resemble "the nations"; she contrives pacts of mutual support with a pagan neighbor—a ploy particularly offensive to the God of Isaiah:

> Woe to the rebellious children,
> says God.
>
> Who carry out plans that are not Mine,
> who weave webs that are not inspired by Me.
>
> Adding sin upon sin.
> They go down to Egypt,
> but My counsel they do not seek.
>
> They find their strength in pharaoh's protection
> and take refuge in Egypt's shadow.
>
> Pharaoh's protection shall be your shame,
> and refuge in Egypt's shadow your disgrace . . . (30:1–3)

✦   ✦   ✦

(Perhaps in this, we make much ado of a small matter. Still, context is everything. Underlying the written word may be a hint—a kind of epiphany, beckoning one behind and beyond the text.)

God's action alas, is all contrary, against the grain of the heart where once it was altogether for, on behalf of—the bloodstream toward and from the heart.

Now we have "wrath . . . detests . . . cast down . . . unmindful . . ." and the strange juxtaposition of "glory cast down" and "footstool."

As though the latter image, applied to the Temple, were not ambiguous at best—a captive crouched, feet of a tyrant resting on a humiliated slave.

Is Israel honored in the image, "footstool of God"? The image hovers uneasily. She is honored and she is not. Her God is God, no tyrant but father, lover, spouse, Whom to serve is highest honor. Human footstool, arise!

✦  ✦  ✦

Start to finish, the mood of the strophe is fiery. The poet treads a furnace. So by implication, are we to walk. "Wrath . . . day of wrath."

Tit for tat is the hideous law of the nations. The world goes mad, Americans set ablaze a conflagration of wrath, the richest nation pulverizes the poorest, Afghanistan.

The media are squeamish and spare us the reality—no images of dying children or fleeing refugees.

✦  ✦  ✦

Fire respects no borders. It has consumed the proud trade towers. The fire next time?

✦  ✦  ✦

PSALM

That from the seed of men
No man,
and from the seed of the olive tree
No olive tree
Shall grow,
This must be measured
With the yardstick of death.

Those who live
Beneath the earth
In cement spheres,
Their strength like
A blade of grass
Lashed by snow.

The desert is history.
Termites write it
Into sand

With their pincers.
And no one will inquire
About a species
Eager
For self-destruction.

(Peter Huchel, *Selected Poems*. Cheadle, England: Carcanet
Press, 1974)

✦   ✦   ✦

**2:2** The image drives on, inexorable, insatiable:

God has consumed without pity
all the dwellings of Jacob;

Has torn down in anger
the fortresses of daughter Juda.

Has brought to ground in dishonor
her kings and her princes.

Is God after all, to be held to accounts? Does the verse refer to grief or
judgment, or something of both? "Without pity . . . in anger . . ." The
emotions are like hands tightening about a throat. They choke off reason.

The losses are cumulative, from rubble to human bones: "dwellings
. . . fortresses . . . kings and princes . . ." One cannot but note that the poet
is charged with the fury he seeks to locate in God.

✦   ✦   ✦

**2:3** Fire again, a leading image of total destruction.

And a God who goes counter, who is single of mind, consuming in
purpose. No longer standing with God's own—implacably against.

What then of the refrain, repeated like a song of sweetness and love, in
the days of creation?

"And God saw that it was good."

Six times repeated, in favor of light (Genesis 1:4) of earth and seas
(1:10), of vegetation (1:12), again of light (1:18), of living creatures twice
(1:21, 25).

And culminating in the human, with a superlative approval upon all:

And God
saw

everything
God
had made,

and
behold,
it was
very
good. (1:31)

✦   ✦   ✦

But Who stands before us now, this incendiary Deity, the Agent of anti-creation?

God broke off in fiery wrath,
the horn that was Israel's whole strength;

Withheld the support of right hand
when the enemy approached,

blazed up in Jacob like a burning fire
devouring all about.

✦   ✦   ✦

There is a midrash on Lamentations in which Moses upbraids God, saying: "Lord of the universe, you have written in your torah":

Whether it be a cow or a ewe, you shall not kill it and
its young both on one day. (Leviticus 22:28)

But they have killed many, many mothers and sons, and you are silent.

✦   ✦   ✦

**2:4** We have a new, unprecedented likeness, with what daring, what mad faith set down:

Like an enemy God made taut the bow,
with arrows in right hand,

Took a stand as a foe, and slew
all on whom the eye doted;

over the tent of daughter Zion,
poured out wrath like fire.

Another notable, even frightening irony. The victimized one is at wisdom and wit's end. Apparently, roles are reversed—perhaps irrevocably. The Friend of creation and covenant, the Spouse of the Song of Songs, has become—"the Enemy." The steadfast Lover, Protector, Provider of manna and water in the wilderness, the Shekinah of the wandering years, is now—"the Foe."

Daring, risky faith! Thus does this unaccountable God appear to the defeated exiles.

✦  ✦  ✦

The modern, technological, universal solvent of human conflicts is—bombing, incursion, sanctions. Destroy people, and so solve human contentions.

Another poet quailed under American fury, taking refuge in shelters in Hanoi, 1968:

BOMBARDMENT

Like those who go aground
willfully, knowing our absurd
estate can but be bettered
in the battering hands of the gods—

yet mourning traitorously the sun and moon,
beloved faces and heat of hearth—

went under
like a blown match. The gases flare on the world's
combustible                                    flesh.

(DB)

✦  ✦  ✦

**2:5** The woman-victim is lost, bereft, shocked. Shall she absorb the catastrophe, and go on? Easier said than done!

She has known much of enmities—how else could that "glory" have arisen, except through wars and a prevailing most costly?

Still, amid chaos and carnage, the heavens stood firm. God was with her.

Or so it was said, and affirmed by priests. So too, the grand liturgies of the sanctuary assured.

Now all, all is changed. The heavens have fallen. God has declared war against the once "chosen."

And the threnody of loss and alienation continues, obsessively.

✦     ✦     ✦

God has become an enemy,
has consumed Israel;

Consumed her castles,
destroyed her fortresses;

For daughter Juda
has multiplied
moaning and groaning.

✦     ✦     ✦

Memory scalds. Can the defeated so much as dream of recovering former glories, will they see once again the beloved horizons of home?

More tormenting by far—will their God ever again be known as Friend, Brother, Lover, Spouse? Can the exiles again befriend their God, and stand, confident, befriended?

✦     ✦     ✦

The questions need not hang on the air like a sword suspended.

For Christians, at a stroke Someone has answered: "Yes. Stand confident, befriended."

Someone has healed and reconciled and died, that the Yes! may live on:

As the Father
has loved Me,

so
I have loved
you.

Live on
in My love . . .

This
is My commandment;

love one another
as I

have loved you.

There is
no greater love
than this;
to lay down
one's life
for one's friends . . .

I
call you
friends,

since I
made known
to you

all

I heard

from
My
Father . . . (John 15:9, 12–13, 15)

✦   ✦   ✦

**2:6–7** The Temple is no more, the holy ceremonies are vanished like a dream of beatitude in a bleak dawn.

And Who, Who has brought the unthinkable to pass? Who shouts a word of doom—nothing safe, nothing sacred!

✦   ✦   ✦

Say it. This God has gone too far, like a Vandal has invaded sacred places, violated sacred persons. The holy vessels, untouchable except by anointed priests, were dealt with like scorpions clinging to a vestment. With a gesture of disdain, God cast them down and down.

God has demolished God's shelter
like a garden booth,

has destroyed
His own dwelling;

Has the sacred been contemned, named anew as profane? It has;

In Zion God has made
feast and sabbath forgotten,

has scorned in fierce wrath
both king and priest.

✦   ✦   ✦

But, but—a corrective. The love turned to loathing, the destruction wrought—these are hardly to be thought arbitrary.

Jeremiah drew a firm indictment and cast it abroad, a net wide as the world:

As the thief is shamed when caught,
so shall the house of Israel be shamed;

they, their kings and their princes,
their priests and their prophets;

they who say to a piece of wood;
"You are my father,"
and to a stone;
"You gave me birth."

They turn to Me their backs,
not their faces;

yet in their time of trouble,
they cry out;
"Rise up and save us!" (2:26–27)

And what of the famed Temple, the sacrifices, the priesthood? Again, to the indictment.

The following message came to Jeremiah from God:

Stand at the gate of the house of God and there proclaim this message; Hear the word of God, all you of Juda who enter these gates to worship God.

Thus says the God of Israel;

Reform your ways and your deeds, so that I may remain with you in this place. Put not your trust in deceitful words; "this is the temple of God, the temple of God, the temple of God!"

Only if you thoroughly reform your ways and your
deeds; if each of you deals justly with your neighbor, if
you no longer oppress the resident alien, the orphan and
the widow; if you no longer shed innocent blood in this
place, or follow strange gods to your harm, will I remain
with you in this place . . ." (7:1–7)

✦ ✦ ✦

**2:7** From crime to consequence. Down with the idolatrous nest.
Let the place resound with pagan shouts of triumph:

God has disowned the altar,
rejected the sanctuary;

the walls of her towers
has handed over to the enemy

who shout in the house of God
as on a feast day.

✦ ✦ ✦

Destruction of the city—a first act.
Exile to follow? Yes.
This must be understood, the consummate irony. It was in grand Jerusalem that the people brought a sea change on themselves. They became a
species of domestic exiles, alienated from truth, strangers to their tradition, to one another, to God.
Scripture clarifies Scripture. Once more Jeremiah, the faithful witness:

When they ask, "Why has God done all these things
to us?" say to them;
"As you have forsaken Me to serve strange gods in
your own land, so shall you serve strangers in a land not
your own." (5:18–19)

✦ ✦ ✦

**2:8** The image here is of a "measuring line," a device for accurate
construction. But wait.
Here, it becomes a tool of precise destruction. And *ecolo*, it lies in the
hand of God—no longer architect of the creation, but its skilled and determined destroyer:

God marked for destruction
the wall of daughter Zion,

stretched out the measuring line—
a hand brought ruin, but did not relent—
brought grief on wall and rampart
till both succumbed.

Isaiah, and the same image:

God will measure her
with line and plummet
to be an empty waste
for satyrs to dwell in. (34:11)

And from Amos, an endearing, all-but-human image, of God the Worker:

Then God showed me this, standing by a wall, a plummet in hand.

God asked me; "What do you see, Amos?" And when I answered,

"A plummet," God said;

"See, I will lay the plummet
against my people Israel.

"I will forgive them
no longer.

"The high places of Isaac
will be laid waste,

and the sanctuaries of Israel
made desolate . . ." (7:7–9)

✦   ✦   ✦

**2:9** A strophe of vulnerability and destitution.

Have we reached the nadir of loss? It would seem so, until we touch on yet another wound . . .

The ramparts are toppled, an image of soul. And what is to become of us? What have we become, but starving mendicants?

Leaderless, rudderless we are. Torah and Prophecy are snatched away.

These were our manna in the world's wilderness, food for survival—and more than survival—celebration of our Emmanuel!

> Sunk into the ground are her gates,
> God has removed and broken her bars.

> Her king and her princes are among the pagans;
> priestly instruction is wanting.
> And her prophets have received
> no vision from God.

✦ ✦ ✦

In this awful winter of '01, "No priestly instruction" and "no vision" from God.

The following letter to the president of the United States Catholic bishops was written by a Jesuit theologian:

> Many, many people wonder why so many of our bishops and cardinals are not expressing the same concern for defenseless human life in Afghanistan, Pakistan and Iraq, as they did in defending the lives of four-day old embryos.
>
> Why are you and your brothers not invoking the principle of sanctity of life? Why do you not invoke the language of the option for the poor? Why do we not see any reference to . . . the Gospels? . . .
>
> Would that we had a voice like Dorothy Day's, which would remind you, our bishops, to remember what happens when you not only fail to criticize but actually support the U.S. administration, as it wages a war that harms and kills many poor civilians . . . (James F. Keenan, S.J.)

✦ ✦ ✦

EVEN PRECISION BOMBING KILLS SOME CIVILIANS, TOUR OF A CITY SHOWS

> Kandahar, Afghanistan, Dec. 25. American and anti-Taliban soldiers entered the city earlier this month, only after the Taliban and Al Qaeda had fled . . .
>
> Muhammad Ismail sat on a wall of his house, where his wife and son were killed when the house next door, where Arabs were staying, was bombed. (*New York Times*)

✦  ✦  ✦

Total war. The media are mobilized, and fall in line. The war demands the brutalizing or numbing of every segment:

> CNN Chair Walter Isaacson ordered his staff to "balance" images of civilian devastation in Afghan cities with reminders that the Taliban harbors murderous terrorists, saying it "seems perverse to focus too much on the casualties or hardship in Afghanistan." In a memo, he admonished reporters covering civilian deaths not to "forget it is that country's rulers who are responsible for the situation Afghanistan is now in" . . .
>
> As "Fairness and Accuracy in Media" puts it, if anything is perverse, "it's that one of the world's most powerful news outlets has instructed its journalists not to report Afghan civilian casualties without attempting to justify those deaths."
>
> CNN has effectively mandated that pro-U.S. propaganda be included in the news, while rationalizing its decision to ignore the genocide looming ahead.
>
> The story is the same at Fox, where news anchor Brit Hume recently wondered why journalists should bother covering civilian deaths. "The question I have" (sic), he said, "is civilian casualties are historically part of war. Should they be as big news as they've been?"
>
> Others, including NPR's Mara Liasson and *U.S. News & World Report's* Michael Barone, go further, arguing that civilian deaths aren't news at all.
>
> What is? Apparently, wild speculation on every imaginable catastrophe, keeping viewers in a permanent state of anxiety—and hopefully, glued to the tube for the next live disaster. (Greg Guma, "Toward Freedom")

✦  ✦  ✦

**2:10–11** Read and weep.

These are the indices of all that has gone awry, has come to naught—suffering innocents: maidens, the aged, children, and mothers. Their protectors, the kings and nobles, are in captivity. So with tradespeople and farmers, the producers of food and services.

Left behind are the unproductive, not worth transporting. Let them languish and die; in our Bible too, these are the "collateral damage" of a wicked system.

✦   ✦   ✦

Careful—we pause and ponder these "lives of no value." They are presented to us as valuable, indeed irreplaceable instructors. Certainly not as images of numb despair.

Do they seem inert, do they lack the will to "do something," to take up their own cause?

Their cause, if we but know it, is our own.

We have missed the point. The aged and the maidens are images of rightful, expedient lamentation.

The atrocious engines of war have left them behind, useless to its rake's progress. Which precisely they are: useless to the prospering of war and warmakers.

In a world gone to ruin, these are assigned—a vocation.

Beyond tasks, beyond usefulness, beyond words. They mourn amid the killers and the killing fields.

Their task is godlike. It is our task as well.

> On the ground in silence sit
> the old men of daughter Zion;
>
> They strew dust on their heads
> and gird themselves with sackcloth;
>
> The maidens of Jerusalem
> bow their heads to the ground. (2:10)

✦   ✦   ✦

**2:11–12** Let the mournful poet at last speak for herself, speak of what her eyes light on with horror—the death of children.

The scene invites a gloss—a scene in Baghdad, the mothers, the dying children, in this awful decade of "sanctions." Or the mothers of Kandahar, as the bombs rain down and children die.

A secretary of state, questioned as to the horrific cost exacted of the people of Iraq through American sanctions, infamously answered, "We think they are worth the price." But who pays and pays? And shall we Americans not pay, shall we pay nothing?

We shall. We did, in New York and Pennsylvania and Washington, D.C., in September of 2001.

✦   ✦   ✦

It might be the mother of a dying child who speaks. Certainly it is a woman, "uselessly" mourning, amid the inarticulate and bereft.

In the wreckage and chaos, her voice is nobly human. And we are grateful:

> Worn out from weeping are my eyes,
> within me all is in ferment;
>
> My gall is poured out on the ground
> because of the downfall of the daughter of my people,
>
> as child and infant faint away
> in the open spaces of the city.
>
> They ask their mothers,
> "Where is the cereal?"—in vain,
>
> as they faint like the battle-wounded
> in the streets of the city,
>
> and breathe their last
> in their mothers' arms.

✦  ✦  ✦

An unexpected, heartrending touch—the dying children are a world apart. They of all victims should not die.

Yet in one awful respect, they resemble the Assyrian or Israeli warriors. Soldiers and infants alike perish.

✦  ✦  ✦

**2:13** Concede it, welcome it, the impasse. Narratives, tropes, poetry—words, words, words fall short. Hands drop helplessly. One can only—be. Be present; bear witness.

If anything can be salvaged of meaning amid the absurd, the debris of hope, it is by way of questioning.

For the moment, seek nothing of right reason or logic or linkage of act and consequence. These go nowhere.

Stand or kneel or lie prone or wander witless, stalemated. Like Job, question existence itself:

> To what shall I liken or compare you,
> O daughter Jerusalem?
>
> What example can I show for your comfort,
> virgin daughter Zion?

> For great as the sea is your downfall;
> Who can heal you?

✦  ✦  ✦

Only an utterly generalized metaphor, stupendous, all but nameless, shoreless, stretching to the verge of the world ("great as the sea")—only this gives access to your plight.

What has befallen is vast (sea of tears?), dumb. It was created on the second day of Genesis, beyond measure or imagining (but not totally beyond).

And here, in effect, an attempt to measure the measureless: "the sea."

✦  ✦  ✦

**2:14** Prophets? No help in that direction. Many among them played toady to an inhuman system, in servitude to illusion. Blind leaders of the blind; no wonder the people strayed!

Far better had there been none of these, and we left to make our way as best (or worst) we might.

✦  ✦  ✦

Our threnody must be accounted a tardy enlightenment. As such, can the awakening be useful, serving not for deepened bitterness, but as occasion for remorse?

Further questions; was not the daughter willingly led astray? Were not true and mighty prophets at hand, as well as false? Were the people not warned, did not Isaiah, Jeremiah, Ezekiel speak up?

Priests, scribes, pseudo-prophets—the true prophets shouted—all fell abominably short. With malice aforethought, avenues of spiritual understanding were blocked:

> The priests asked not,
> "Where is God?"

> Those who dealt with the law
> knew Me not;

> The shepherds
> rebelled against Me.

> The prophets prophesied by Baal
> and went after useless idols. (2:8)

✦  ✦  ✦

**2:14** After so scorching a diatribe, comes judgment:

> Your prophets had for you
> false and specious visions;
> They did not lay bare your guilt,
> to avert your fate;
>
> They beheld for you in vision
> false and misleading portents.

✦   ✦   ✦

And what of the words of great Isaiah, who glories in terrifying ironies and oppositions?

Stunningly, in image after image, he set down the psychology of mordant self-will.

Be as you are, urges God. Be the worst, work at it handily. Become skilled at being the worst, become the very best of the worst:

> Be irresolute, stupefied;
> blind yourselves and stay blind!
>
> Be drunk, but not with wine,
> stagger, but not from strong drink!
>
> For God has poured out on you
> a spirit of deep sleep,
>
> has shut your eyes, the prophets,
> and covered your heads, the seers.

Be alert now for dark, saving intricacies. Quick as a wink, Isaiah reveals the sleight of hand and eye, the slippery evasion:

> For you the revelation of all this has become like the words of a sealed scroll. When it is handed to one who can read, with the request, "Read this," he replies, "I cannot; it is sealed."
> When it is handed to one who cannot read, with the request, "Read this," he replies, "I cannot read."
> (29:9–12)

✦   ✦   ✦

**2:15–17** Let the worst come, let the heavens fall. Only then shall we see the hand of God, when we reel under it, blow by blow.

Into the scene of wreckage, more or less guilty bystanders venture, the tourists of tragedy. These see—and see nothing. They know neither loss nor pain.

Uninvolved, neutral, they gesture, a more or less magical effort to ward off the fate they dread:

> All who pass by
> clap their hands at you;
> They hiss and wag their heads
> over daughter Jerusalem;
>
> "Is this the all-beautiful city,
> the joy of the whole earth?"

✦   ✦   ✦

The ethical neuters yield to worse enemies.

These are, one surmises, the Babylonians; or perhaps the Edomites or Moabites, or those perennial troublemakers, the Philistines. Or the Egyptians.

Enemies everywhere, as Isaiah testifies. And as in a mirror image, enemy sees enemy. And see peering, daughter Jerusalem sheds her tenderness.

She dons armor and sword, a very David, a warrior supreme. Which is to say and say again, to see and see again, as in a glass darkly—an enemy among enemies.

Under that rubric, a rancorous delight erupts in the despairing and fallen.

The close resemblance, the violence! Whether in the vanquished or conqueror, or the more or less guilty bystanders—hostility, for the moment, no will to forgive and start over.

We touch on the nadir of mourning—a vengeance that goes nowhere.

And yet, vengeance erupts. It must be given place and a hearing— even as it must be renounced. Giving it place in Lamentations is an assurance that our instincts, even those we find shameful, are not forbidden. They are respected. Then they yield to the strong corrective of Christ.

Give it time and place, then, rancor, revenge.

We need it. That mirror again; ourselves, the image in the glass:

> All your enemies
> open their mouths against you;
>
> They hiss and gnash their teeth.
> They say; "We have devoured her.

"this at last is the day we hoped for;
we have lived to see it."

The words lie like a smear of blood across the pages of our scripture. In these days of fierce enmity, in the winter of discontent, '01 and its war of plain vengeance, can we ignore such awful words?

It would perhaps be to our comfort, the comfort of amnesia.

No, we need reminding, lest we fall to mindlessness.

Words of ungovernable malice are quoted by an omniscient observer. And the words, together with the mood that forms them, are native, North American, home grown.

The fuses are lit over Afghanistan, the huge bombs discharge. Americans exult in yet another military victory, the defeat of the demonized Taliban.

But. Every bomb that falls is a dragon's tooth, sown in the furrows of the tormented earth. Only give them time!

The topless towers of Manhattan lie smoldering, stinking with corpses. Will not worse come of this misbegotten misadventure?

Jerusalem, Nov. 25, '01. Terrorism cannot be combated successfully unless the worsening disparities between the rich and the poor are addressed, said the president of Pax Christi International.

"The only solution lies in social justice," said Patriarch Michel Sabbah, Latin-rite patriarch of Jerusalem. . . . "We must recognize that global disparity is fundamentally incompatible with global security" . . . (*National Jesuit News*, 12/01)

**2:17** Once more we hear from the ambivalent mourners, their divided mind. The disaster is of God; no, it is of the enemy.

Can it be that God has become the primal enemy, has nudged into fury against God's own, the mighty war machine of Assyria?

Again we turn to Isaiah, in poetry and narrative a truthful witness of the time of testing.

God speaks:

Against an impious nation I send him,
and against a people under My wrath I order him

to seize, plunder, carry off loot,
and tread them down like the mud of the streets . . .

as My hand reached out to idolatrous kingdoms
that had more images than Jerusalem and Samaria,
just as I treated Samaria and her idols,
shall I not do to Jerusalem and her graven images?
(10:6, 10, 11)

✦  ✦  ✦

The voice of conscience is one with the voice of God. And this none too soon, one thinks with relief.

Long before catastrophe struck, unity had frayed. The chosen worshipped and worshipped, panoply and priestcraft, spectacle and procession. It stank in God's nostrils.

We knew what Ezekiel and Isaiah made of it—a religion without soul, devoid of justice and compassion. A heap of filthy straw set aflame, a stench.

God speaks:

"It is you
who devoured the vineyard;

the loot
wrested from the poor

lies
in your house.

What do you mean
by crushing My people,

grinding down the poor,
when they look
to you?"

says
the God

of
hosts. (Isaiah 3:14–15)

✦  ✦  ✦

First the decree, then the act. Relentless, tight logic from on high—crime and consequence.

Only a few acknowledged the systemic sin, and these were invariably scorned.

As to consequence, a few quaked in their bones; we name them prophets.

In verse 17 we encounter crime and consequence. Our mourner knows of these only amid filth, rubble, and the void:

> God has done as decreed,
> has fulfilled the threat
>
> set forth from days of old,
> has destroyed and had no pity,
>
> letting the enemy gloat over you,
> and exalting the horn of your foes.

## chapter three

# "The rod of God's anger . . .
# My fill of wormwood . . ." (2:18–3:45)

**2:18–19** Urging the daughter to "cry out," the author cries out.

And in an adroit literary ploy, the tears he urges are not his own. But of course they are his own, and by every right.

It was (s)he, poet and prophet, who in dark apprehension walked before the catastrophe, a sure guide, and spoke and ranted before. Sin and consequence, sin and consequence! This the task, the vocation—though few gave heed:

> God said:
> since this people draws near
> with words only
>
> and honors Me
> with its lips only,
>
> their hearts are far from Me,
> and their reverence for me
>
> has become a routine observance
> of the precepts of humans.
>
> Therefore
> I will deal
> with this people
>
> in surprising
> and wondrous fashion;
>
> The wisdom
> of the wise
> shall perish
>
> and the understanding
> of the prudent

shall
be
hid. (Isaiah 29:13–14)

✦   ✦   ✦

So, even late, they weep; better, all said, than no tears at all. Better a tardy change of heart, than a heart of stone intact amid the rubble.

And one senses in the present dialog, a law in place. What is urged of others (if rightly so, in accord with humane reason) is first undergone. Mutuality, mingling of tears, a communion:

> Cry out to God,
> moan, O daughter Zion
>
> Let your tears flow like a torrent
> day and night;
>
> let there be no respite for you,
> no repose for your eyes. (Lamentations 2:18)

The day is too short for lamenting. Night must fall, it brings no respite; let the lamentation go on.

Indeed night is the proper climate and color of grief. No sun in sky or in soul, no relief, a veil of darkness over all, blank, void, death.

The soul is turned to water, hydrated to tears. Pure grief, it flows, loses substance and proper form. Gone is the sense of "I am."

But wait—Someone puts to naught that "blank, void, death." A Someone undeclared, whose Presence is veiled, dark, in form, named, if named at all—Absence:

> Rise up, shrill in the night,
> at the beginning of every watch;
>
> pour out your heart like water
> in the presence of God . . . (Lamentations 2:19)

In the same strophe, we come to a kind of instruction. What, whom to pray for in such times, such perpetual night, its "every watch"?

It is the children; the daughter Zion is also mother Jerusalem. Suddenly lamentation pauses, alert, takes form and content.

That soul of hers had turned to water in the night. But no—she hears the wail of a child, and reclaims herself.

My soul, my children! She is transformed, she heeds the call, begs for the lives of the endangered and innocent:

> . . . lift up your hands to God
> for the lives of your little ones
>
> who faint from hunger
> at the corner of every street.

✦　✦　✦

In the iron age of war, an iron law is promulgated; it is the children who die first. War is mass cannibalism; we eat our own future. In the horrid banquet, all, victor and vanquished, have sordid part.

War brings onset of madness, denial of sweet instinct and caring.

Mothers are hardest stricken. A morbid drama is assigned them—the act of giving birth is one with the act of dealing death.

Courageously, awfully, our Lamentation takes war and consequence in account. The urging of the poet-prophet is heeded; lament becomes a last-ditch petition:

> Hear O God, and consider;
> whom have You ever treated thus?
>
> Must women eat their offspring,
> their well-formed children? . . .

✦　✦　✦

The scene is atrociously illustrated in the sanctions imposed against the children—in effect, first against them—of Iraq. As has been testified again and again. The children are denied food and medical care, and they die in great numbers.

Statistics of shame are rendered shameless by a remark that refuses to die on the air. Secretary Albright, questioned as to the matter, famously responded; "We think they (the sanctions) are worth the price."

Which was apt, in a perverse way, since those who so weigh human lives against power, seldom if ever are called to pay up.

The "daughter Zion" of our Lamentation is also "mother Jerusalem."

The Secretary, it appears, is hardly to be thought either. She is cannibalistic, a warrior justifying her kind.

✦　✦　✦

**2:20** We come at length to cases; they invite the above reflection.

War is a monstrous cannibal. Our text so to speak, makes no bones of it.

✦  ✦  ✦

Another text spells the matter out, in straight narration and horrendous detail, one of the most daunting stories in our Bible (2 Kings 6:28 ff).

Samaria is under siege. The war has come home to roost like a carrion bird. Pretense and imperial rhetoric and the purported will of Jawe notwithstanding, women and children and the aged and unborn are tossed about, somewhere between earth and hell, jumbled in a sack of misery, slung over the shoulder of warrior Mars.

If the innocent cannot be outright disposed of, there remains another method to the same end. Starve them.

Our story opens. Seeking relief from stench and smoke, the king walks the ramparts of the stricken city, alone.

And a woman approaches, distraught, crying out: "Help, lord king!"

We take note, and are startled; the king and the woman are unnamed. A king, nameless? But the entire book is named for the Kings!

The omission is as remarkable as would be the naming of the woman.

The woman raises her piteous cry. The king, exasperated, yells into the wind, like the bellow of a struck bullock: "May God help you not at all! Where is my help to come from—would it be from a rock or a hard place?"

Nonetheless his heart is moved. Compassion stirs, half unwilling: "What is your trouble?"

As if he did not know her trouble; as if her trouble were not his own!

The woman pours out her tale of woe. A few days previous, a friend, a mother like herself, approached with a horrifying proposal.

This: starving as we are, today we will slay and eat one of our children, yours. And on the morrow, likewise my child.

That day they ate their horrid fill. And on the day following, his woman approached her friend. But the friend reneged, and hid her infant.

Our story is of wartime; we sup of horrors. The abysmally abnormal is rendered—normal.

✦  ✦  ✦

In another Scripture, a nightmarish imagery. An invitation is issued to a horrid banquet. The menu:

the flesh
of all,

free
and slave,

small
and
great. (Revelation 19:17–18)

From the banquet, we pass to a battlefield. John the seer, imprisoned on the island of Patmos, speaks:

I saw
the beast

and the kings
of earth,

and the armies
they mustered,

to do
battle

with
the One

who rode
the horse. (verse 19)

✦  ✦  ✦

The rich nations sit to table. Their menu? The children of the poor nations. Banquet and battle are mutual metaphors. In the course (sic) of contending for economic domination, fair means or foul, no matter. Children become grist for the Insatiable Great Gut.

For more then a decade, the innocents of Iraq are served up.

✦  ✦  ✦

Our story of the siege of Samaria ends with the king rending his garments in despair.

Still, matters do not end there. Despair is never the intent of a biblical story—quite the opposite.

The woman's wild tale, the king's helplessness, burn on the page, as though self-combusting. For our sake.

His lonely pacing, the woman's threnody—we ponder the text, as multitudes have done before us. The ancient siege, the distraught king, the two women (where is the second, what has become of her?), the children doomed.

✦ ✦ ✦

Two kings frame the story: The king besieged and the king leading the assault, winner and loser alike; each is unnamed, an indistinguishable clichè. Someone wins, someone loses, the old wearying game.

And we mourn the wars of the centuries since, the wars of our lifetime, the wars searing the bones of every continent.

Even as these notes are set down, the bloodbath is steeped, from Manhattan to Afghanistan.

✦ ✦ ✦

Enlarge the question. To a sane mind, has there been in any war a victor, in any civilized, recognizable sense? Which is to ask, Did the victors in virtue of prevailing, emerge sober and compassionate, determined on "war, never again"?

Impossible. It was always, "war, ever again!"

Were they (which is to way, we), further brutalized and bent toward yet another bloodletting?

Will the orgy stop only when time stops, and the last human is vaporized?

✦ ✦ ✦

**2:21–22** The holy in guise of blasphemy, devotion in the form of accusation; are we not in the realm of the faith/unfaith of a Job?

Which is to say, if we dare venture it—are we not in the realm of biblical faith?

Once more the pendulum swings; from confession of guilt to judgment against God. You, You, You. It is horrendous, it is true:

> dead in the dust of the streets
> lie young and old;
>
> My maidens and young men
> have fallen by the sword;
>
> You have slain on the day of Your wrath
> slaughtered without pity. (Lamentations 2:21)

"My enemy." And in context, left unclear. Is the enemy Assyrian warriors, is the enemy God? Are the two in fact one, the mortal foe spurred on by the divine?

What an image! The "enemy" (that word again), as if to make a holi-
day, in horrid glee descended on the city. This was total war, without pity
or mercy:

> You summoned as for a feast day
> terror against me from all sides;
>
> There was not, on the day of Your wrath
> either fugitive or survivor;
>
> those whom I bore and reared,
> my enemy has utterly destroyed. (Lamentations 2:22)

✦   ✦   ✦

In chapter 3, one immediately notes a change of pace, a new stylistic
device. In place of the simple acrostics of chapters 1, 2, 4, and 5, we have
here an extension. Grief, lament is wracked, stretched out; instead of a
single verse assigned to a Hebrew letter, we have three verses for each.

Our present chapter is the "unwobbling pivot" of the book.

Or it is like the probe of a surgeon. It searches every corner of grief,
puts the shadows to rout, faces the ghosts of memory. It lingers over the
interstices and tegument of sorrow—sixty-six verses in all.

The communal voice of the other chapters yields. No longer do "daughter Jerusalem," "mother Zion" complain and plead. Here one mourner
only, one voice lamenting.

We have met this figure of loss before. The one lamenting is the "I" of
Job, or the suffering servant of Second Isaiah, or Jeremiah in the pit. He is
Jesus in the days of His passion (Caravaggio, that errant genius, caught
Him close).

Woman or man (woman more often abused, more deadly dealt with,
more contemned and scapegoated)—*eccolo*, we have here the innocent of
every time and place, walking the fires.

The innocents of our time and place, of the World Trade towers crushing their human cargo. The Afghan peasants fleeing, as the obscene
bombers prowl like sharks of the upper air.

God forgive us.

✦   ✦   ✦

**3:1–3** No ambiguity here, the plunge. The images are devastating, the
tongue is of Job.

> I am one who has known affliction
> from the rod of God's anger;

> one whom God has led and forced to walk
> in darkness, not in the light;

> against me alone God brings down a hand
> again and again, all the day.

✦  ✦  ✦

"J' accuse!" God is summoned to the dock. We hear a muffled drumbeat of affliction: "Against me alone . . . again and again."

The rod, a forced march in darkness, the punishing swipe of a hand; how dare the mourner utter such words?

Dangerous—and how distant we are from conventional religiosity!

This, the word of God? Summon the friends of Job and their deadly pieties, their suffocating deity of jot and tittle. Let them raise the cry: blasphemy.

✦  ✦  ✦

**3:4–6** Again, the haunting image of darkness and death. As though death would come (if only it would come!) as relief.

But alas for the elusive rescuer—death is long in coming.

What remains is death as mirage, metaphor. God has gone ruthlessly counter:

> God has worn away my flesh and my skin,
> has broken my bones,

> has beset me round about
> with poverty and weariness,

> has left me to dwell in the dark
> like those long dead.

✦  ✦  ✦

**3:7–9** What does not fail is the fierce, primal vitality of the poetry.

The images shift. They bespeak prayer lost in a whirlwind of chaos. Or they summon a prisoner, boxed in. Or one bedeviled, bewildered, whose paths have twisted into a labyrinth, with no out.

Does he pray for deliverance? He does, and to no avail. He cries out in the teeth of contrary winds. They mock his anguish, make sport of his plea.

Has the human plight—the plight of the just—been explored more terrifyingly, even by Job?

God has hemmed me in with no escape,
weighed me down with chains;

even when I cry out for help,
God stops my prayer,

blocks my way with fitted stones,
turns my paths aside.

✦  ✦  ✦

**3:10–11** Make no mistake, this God is like a ravening beast on the prowl. He (sic) would kill, consume me utterly.

I must evade His lethal will, must feint and weave about, lost. Another kind of death! He leaves me bewildered, unsure of the right way.

JPS is relentlessly physical:

He has forced me off my way, and mangled me.
A lurking bear He has been to me,
a lion in ambush!

He deranged my ways, set me astray,
left me desolate.

✦  ✦  ✦

**3:12–13** Losses, losses—and this surfeit of poetry. Surely the images are meant to be drawn on again and again, waters from the deep well of grace, as we make our sorry way through a Fallen creation.

Be it noted too, that the technological supermen are lacking in a crucial skill. To such, our book is a hieroglyphic; they know nothing of lamentation. Grieve, for what, for whom? Ours is a just cause . . .

Moral boundaries have dissolved. They own creation and human lives, to dispose of or to spare, as it serves their interests.

They inflict violent death on multitudes, and call the crime "collateral damage." And the creation languishes under their bombings and assaults.

✦  ✦  ✦

Our poet, thank God, knows much of *lacrimae rerum*, "the tears of things."

Tell us more then, crowd the page with living images!

Who is this God? Help us, poet!

God cannot be thrown off; the tracking, the pursuit goes on. God is a warrior, an archer; and I alas, the prey. Skilled, sure, God is a pathfinder, silent as an Iroquois scout.

The pain pierces to the gut, just short of lethal. The seer lives, but barely, to tell of it.

God has allowed this? Let us syncopate the assault; God has wrought this:

> God bent the bow and set me up
> as target for an arrow.
>
> God pierces my sides with shafts from the quiver.

✦  ✦  ✦

The "light unto the nations" is quenched. And what of that one who

> shall
> bring forth
>
> justice
>
> to
> the
> nations?

What of that promise, spoken to the chosen:

> I,
> God,
>
> have called
> you
>
> for
> the victory
>
> of
> justice
>
> I have grasped
> you
> by the hand,
>
> I formed
> you,
>
> and set
> you

as a covenant
of the people,

a light
for the nations . . . (Isaiah 42:6)

✦   ✦   ✦

**3:14–19** Nothing remains of this noble vocation of bearing the truth of God's justice on winds of time. Nothing. The promise is in tatters, fortune is reversed, lamentable, total.

Demoralized, what now can one offer the nations? Life is a poisoned cup. Drink to the lees!

Or perhaps one seeks solid nourishment? No manna for you, no storm of sweetness and plenty.

The skies are a *tabula rasa*. Fall to ground, eat the stones your foot falls on:

I have become a laughingstock for all nations,
their taunt all the day long.

God has sated me with bitter food,
made me drink my fill of wormwood.

God has broken my teeth with gravel,
pressed my face in the dust.

✦   ✦   ✦

Hands drop. The images fall short in the telling.

Before our eyes is a poetry of exhaustion, ever so slowly traced by a failing pen. The soul wanders in its dark night.

Darkness-soul, one substance.

And who can know the true way, or walk there?

Walk where? Its name is—Nowhere. At wit and wisdom's end, you barely stand, barely exist.

Concede it. Surrender. Dare embrace it—near nothing. Yourself.

My soul is deprived of peace,
I have forgotten what happiness is.

I tell myself, my future is lost,
all that I hoped for from God.

"All I hoped for." This is our own story, necessarily in past tense, this delay, this hope deferred, lifelong. We hoped for peace, we wrote and belabored the theme, we longed for nothing else, years and years. We vigiled and marched and crossed lines and were arrested, tried and disposed of in kangaroo courts and jails across the land.

In 2001, I turned eighty. That same year, the twin towers fell in Manhattan, and another American saga of revenge opened. The state mobilized mightily, the Church fell in line.

"All I had hoped for." The world has fallen to a brutal scramble, more atrocious, more thwarting to sane understanding than when we began the work of peacemaking.

And our beloved Church? It has become the spiritual arm of thuggish warmongers.

Surrender. Dare embrace it. Near nothing. Yourself.

✦　✦　✦

**3:20** We have seen it, endured it, the questioning of God, of the worth of our own existence. Where to venture, to turn?

A low mood, mulling things over and over. And there comes neither respite nor relief. Something other—bitterness on the tongue. One has tasted obscenity:

> The thought of my homeless poverty
> is wormwood and gall,
>
> remembering it over and over
> leaves my soul downcast within me.

✦　✦　✦

Then, at long last there comes, amid the doom and gloom of actual life (and of our Lamentation)—such relief as brings tears. Relief in a landscape long devoid of hope.

A pendulum swings; the absence of God, the killing darkness, the Hand that withholds and pummels—these yield to the Presence, the Consolation. Start the litany. God is palpable. God takes sides. God stands with the just. God witnesses. God promises. Better, God is Promise.

✦　✦　✦

Throughout the threnody, we had not heard much of hope. What we heard was so tenuous and meager, so aligned with its dark opposite, so beyond touch or reach—we had all but jettisoned the word as a chimera, a no-thing.

Alas for Jerusalem! Every worldly support failed.

The Temple became a befouled nest of idolaters, the palace harbored deeds of infamy.

Both must come down.

But this is penultimate, as Jeremiah was instructed. First things first:

> This day I set you
> over kingdoms and over nations,
>
> to root up
> and to tear down,
>
> to destroy
> and to demolish . . .

That harsh instruction is preliminary. The "No" is to be followed by an even more emphatic "Yes";

> . . . to build
> and to plant. (1:10)

✦  ✦  ✦

Yet another image is dear to the Psalmist, to Isaiah and Amos: the Promise of return.

Images abound; teeming harvests, favor resting on the land and its people. Chastened by exile they return and reclaim the heritage:

> Look, a time is coming,
> declares God—
>
> when the plowman
> will overtake the reaper,
>
> the treader of grapes
> the sower.
>
> The mountains
> will drip wine,
>
> and all the hills
> will melt. (Amos 9:13)

✦  ✦  ✦

Talk about hyperbole—that nice final flourish, as the "mountains drip" and the "hills melt" under a cascade of wine and fruits!

✦　✦　✦

Promise, the Promise! God repeats it to Isaiah:

As I pour water
on parched ground,

rivulets
on dry land,

I will pour
My Spirit
on your seed,

My blessing
on your offspring.

And they will sprout
from amid the grass

like willows
by streams
of water. (44:3–4)

✦　✦　✦

And here, the confident confession of one who has met doubt and darkness face to face, and overcome:

O God, your kindness
reaches to the heavens,

Your faithfulness,
to the clouds.

Your justice
is like the mountains of God;

Your judgments,
like the mighty deep.

How precious
is your kindness, O God!

The children take refuge
in the shadow of Your wings.

They have their fill
of the prime gifts
of Your house

From Your delightful stream You give them
to drink.

For with You
is the fountain
of life,

and
in Your light

we
see
light. (Psalm 35:6–10)

✦　✦　✦

**3:21–30** To our text. And suddenly, words are composed of pure light. No more lamenting—now the mourner can scarcely credit the whispering of his own heart, the words forming under his pen. Words of joy, relief, hope, and the poet transformed.

✦　✦　✦

In verse 21 he begins tentatively, like a little child essaying a first step; or why not?—a second:

to mind

as
my reason

to
have
hope . . .

Then on and on, he breathes freely, confidently. Imagination is in full play. As he walks, he plucks from thin air images, truths:

are not exhausted,

God's mercies
are not spent;

they are renewed
each morning,

so great
is God's faithfulness. (3:22–23)

✦ ✦ ✦

We had not heard the like before. We had heard only a single motif, exploring like a mournful violin every cranny of the stalled heart, a plenum of grief and loss.

Now we are subtly reminded—Lamentation is not the sole response of those who believe and are broken.

Or better—Lamentation also, though rarely and tentatively—smiles.

As here. Come, urges the poet, walk with me out of the night. God is still God, the Promise holds firm.

✦ ✦ ✦

"In my end is my beginning."

What a long way we have come, to arrive at the house where we were born, or reborn.

Events that seemed charged with a killing complexity, a labyrinthine illogic, inducing near despair—at last these are relieved.

Childlike, dare to love, and so embrace the mystery:

> My portion is God,
> says my soul.
>
> Therefore
> will I hope
>
> in
> God. (3:24)

Confess. Then with relief, fall to reflection.

Not to speculation, be it noted, nor to obsession with the ills befalling self or the world. Thankfully, we are done with that (at least for a time!).

While the blessed mood is on us, celebrate, give full play to the Good, suffusing the soul like a sunrise:

> Good is God
> to one who waits
> for God,
>
> to the soul
> that seeks
> God.
>
> It is good
> to hope in silence

for the saving help
of God. (3:25–26)

Let the paradox stand, fruitful, a dark night of the senses.
When nothing can be done, this can be done; this non-doing; "seeking
. . . hoping . . . in silence."

✦   ✦   ✦

November 30, '01 marks the funeral of the 300th New York firefighter
killed in the twin towers. By now, scalding grief has yielded to a blank,
muted acceptance. What must be done, shall be done; due honors.

And the same day, a pastor phones from Connecticut. His voice is flat,
discouraged. He confesses to being at rope's end. Bush's draconian de-
crees, war abroad and repression at home, have denied hope to a good
man. Would I come to his parish, and offer hopeful reflections?

I would. And perhaps we have here in our text, a start.

Neither he nor I can unfix the mask of fascist authority. We must live
through this, salvaging what decency and community we can muster; from
bible, sacrament, one another.

We can "seek . . . hope . . . in silence . . ."

(And refusing to make the good the enemy of the better, we can state
our convictions publicly, prayerfully. "No" to war, to scapegoating, to de-
tention of suspects and military tribunals and the other paraphernalia of
the titans!)

✦   ✦   ✦

Which seems a natural lead to our next strophe, standing unexpected
and austere on the page.

It comes as a reminder; one's humanity is not primarily an inheritance or a gift from on high. Living humanly has a price attached. Let us
pay up, and gladly. Knowing as well that the opposite, living inhumanly,
pays huge dividends in a crooked world.

Celebrate then, the burden.

Paul has named it as a wondrous oxymoron; *pondus gloriae*, "a weight
of glory." A glory to be sure, but a burden as well, as indicated:

It is good
for one
to bear

the yoke
from
youth. (3:27)

✦ ✦ ✦

The yoke of the law; of God's law. And rightly understood, often in conflict with the law of the land.

Whatever of our humanity survives this terrifying century, one thing is certain. Sooner or later (later rather than sooner!), a few friends will be honored as mentors of the art of the human.

For the present, they are in official disgrace, imprisoned for nonviolent acts in opposition against nuclear war.

Upon these, the Plowshares prisoners, the yoke of God's law weighs heavy. Years are exacted of them, they endure punitive courts, transport in chains, isolation from loved ones, denial of prisoners' scant rights, solitary confinement.

Let this text be to them, noble women and men, both comfort and strength:

> Let [her] sit alone and in silence,
> when the yoke is laid upon [her]
>
> Let [her] put mouth to the dust;
> there may yet be hope.
>
> Let [her] offer cheek to be struck,
> let [her] be filled with disgrace. (3:28–30)

✦ ✦ ✦

Up, down, the pendulum of mood swings; and to our advantage. The movement is a sign of life; the one who suffers has not grown numb or calloused. Far from it, he embraces life at its most awful—and most wondrous.

Who is this God, what is God's purpose for the world, for this life of mine? Why do I suffer? Am I caught in a net of guilt, a kind of "roundup" of presumed sinners? Is the image of God as "Fowler" to be accounted true, or a confabulation of low moods?

✦ ✦ ✦

**3:31–34** Let me be jolted out of this unprofitable dudgeon. The God of the Bible, of the prophets, I know that One; God's name is Compassion, Hope!

> For God's rejection
> does not last forever.

> Though God afflicts, God takes pity
> in abundant kindness,
>
> has no joy in afflicting
> or grieving others,
>
> crushing underfoot
> all the prisoners of earth.

(In the last strophe, I follow JPS as both striking and original, rather than NAM, which attributes the "crushing" to wicked humans).

"All the prisoners of earth," a startling synonym for humans as such. Are we prisoners of the Fall, of sin? Or does the name apply only to survivors of the destroyed city, those who were led off to exile? Intriguing.

✦   ✦   ✦

**3:35–36** A hint once more of the "law of the land," and its falling short of the justice of God.

Human law, national law, protect vast areas and weapons given over to works of death.

As for objectors to the system, they must be severely dealt with.

But the text speaks up on behalf of these, even as it overturns official tables, indicting judges, prosecutors, wardens, they and their apparatus of crime and punishment:

> To deny one's rights
> in the very sight of the most High,
>
> to wrong one in his cause,
> this God does not choose.

✦   ✦   ✦

**3:37–39** Our poet takes refuge in a kind of *via media*, a "middle way."

For a start, there is no known way of justifying God vis-à-vis ourselves. Confess it. Great Job did not succeed in the task. He was swamped by an epiphany, saying in effect: "Yield. You succeed only in tormenting yourself and annoying Me."

And what of the friends of Job? They snared the wind in nets, the wind of their own palaver, and called it god.

Their deity, as matters turned, was strictly lower case, second rate.

Where these failed, shall our poet succeed?

He prefers to dissipate the good-evil conundrum, to take refuge in generalities. Good and evil proceed (in some way or other), from God. Leave it at that.

✦ ✦ ✦

And by way of summing up, let us not permit intellectual pride to jettison a sense of sinfulness. Recall and be chastened; if evil befell us, it was because we had conspired with evil.

A vile bargain was struck, in temple, palace, marketplace, battlefield; a ravenous economy and vicious military, secret and socialized idolatry, the "chariots and silver" denounced by Isaiah.

We violated the boundaries of the human, declared ourselves masters of life and death.

✦ ✦ ✦

How chastening to confess; we Americans—our wars, our contempt for the victimized—we are accountable to Another:

> Who commands so that it comes to pass,
> except God ordain it;
>
> except it proceed from the mouth of the most High,
> whether the thing be good or bad!
>
> Why should any living man complain,
> any mortal, in face of his sins?

The final strophe invites a smile. Throughout our book of Lamentations, one of the great complainers of the Bible has taken his place on the dung heap of Job.

And now, he decries with a "why complain?" —even as he enlarges the plaints through an entire book.

Come now, poet!

✦ ✦ ✦

**3:40–42** It is as though winter descended, and we must cross a treacherous stream. The ice has broken up, the current races. And we cross, stepping gingerly from one floe to another.

He refuses to let us off easily, with those verses on God's "mercy . . . favors . . . faithfulness. . ." "Rejoicing in God's compassion" must not induce amnesia. Judgment too is at hand.

Presently, a *scrutatio cordium* resumes, an examen of conscience.

Let us search and examine our ways
that we may return to God!

Let us reach out our hearts
toward God in heaven!

We have sinned and rebelled;
You have not forgiven us.

That last line falls like a whip across the shoulders.

We had read, and been heartened: "mercies unspent . . . favors not exhausted . . . God takes pity . . . abundance or mercies . . ."

Now we are appalled, even as we are liberated.

In our Bible, there is no "prayerfully correct" way to God. There are as many ways as there are prophets, saints, martyrs, their moods volcanic or pacific, their lives a tragedy, a triumph, a horror.

There is a God, there is mercy as well as judgment. Judgment and mercy; play the themes off, one against the other, one with the other. Terror and confidence, both.

It may be, because one has suffered judgment on earth, the time of mercy has come.

✦   ✦   ✦

Catastrophe strikes, hearts are in turmoil. A poet speaks for all, for himself.

Is there a rule that governs access to the most High? If so, it has a Zen quality, puzzling, generous, oneiric, attentive to our plight.

No procrustean bed here! Let the heart have its say, its rhythms.

✦   ✦   ✦

**3:43–45** We have pondered the story of God in the prophetic books, as well as the story of the god of Samuel and the kings.

In our book, storms belabor the world. A stormy God strikes the holy and innocent alike, curses the chosen, brings the city down.

A tale ancient as Genesis and the deluge. Job had it by heart, and the Psalmist and Isaiah. And with utmost poignancy, Jeremiah.

✦   ✦   ✦

The wild theme enters our poem like a trail of blood under a door. Did we clean the blood, refurbish the room, and summon a God of mercy and hope?

We did—and to small avail.

Blood will have blood. As though to name in a rubric the guilty—the blood returns, the exaction, the judgment:

> You veiled yourself in wrath and pursued us,
> You slew us and took no pity;
>
> You wrapped Yourself in a cloud
> which prayer could not pierce.
>
> You have made us offscouring and refuse
> among the nations.

✦  ✦  ✦

It stops the heart, this fierce indictment—of God.

Item after item, a bill of particulars is drawn up.

Reference to the "cloud" resonates with terrific irony. The "shekinah" led the tribe through the wilderness years, a sign of holy providence. Then at the arrival in Jerusalem, It settled in the Temple of David.

And here, what has become of the image? It grows dense, hardens into a wall, even a kind of hideaway. Within it, by implication God turns His back and stops His ears.

*chapter four*

# "You came to my aid and . . .
# You said, 'have no fear'" (3:46–4:19)

**3:46–48** Enemies, or God the enemy—or both mingled? The people are at sea, our poet clings to a spar and cries out.

✦   ✦   ✦

At sea we are meant to be; to taste something of the fate of the Afghan refugees, as American bombers pummel the moonscape in the awful winter of '01, reducing dust to finer dust. This land, bereft of orchards and vines and forests, land of perennial victims, the women and children and aged trudging a circle of hell.

Or the misfortunate land—is it our own, is it the U.S.? The thought occurs, a properly biblical implication. "Judgment is Mine."

Let the poem borrow the voices of the driven and exiled. Let us mourn for them—and for ourselves as well. For our thrice benighted leaders. Of them, no tears are recorded. "The president is on a roll," is jubilantly recorded.

For the victims, tears and more tears, the human lot in a benighted age.

> Our enemies
> have opened their mouths against us;
>
> terror and the pit have been our lot,
> desolation and destruction;
>
> My eyes run with streams of water
> for the downfall of the daughter of my people.

✦   ✦   ✦

What should not be, what must not be, in accord with every civilized canon—is. Thus the law of empire, as the bombers pummel the sterile plains of the poorest country on earth.

It is winter. The innocent impede the machinery of revenge and retaliation. So they endure the open roads, battered from hither to yon.

✦   ✦   ✦

We call barbarians
people living on the other side of the border.

We call civilized
people living on this side of the border.

We civilized,
living on this side of the border,

are not ashamed
to arm ourselves to the teeth

to protect ourselves
against the barbarians

born on the other side.

And when the barbarians
born on the other side
invade us,

we do not hesitate
to kill them

before
we civilize them.

So the civilized
exterminate barbarians
without civilizing them.

And we persist
in calling ourselves
civilized. (Peter Maurin, "Easy Essays," quoted from
*Catholic Worker*)

✦   ✦   ✦

Falling tears are the timepiece of the poor. Weeping marks the days from the nights, the nights from days, alike in misery.

Still, amid all, a gleam, a Presence. Dare one hope? Can it be that Someone sees, Someone witnesses?

**3:49–51** Dare it!

> My eyes flow without ceasing,
> there is no respite,
>
> till God from heaven
> looks down and sees.
>
> My eyes torment my soul
> at the sight of the daughters of my city.

✦  ✦  ✦

Jeremiah has been scourged, put in the stocks, a laughingstock. Let him die. Ever old and new, it is the same argument and charge:

> "This man ought to be put to death," the princes said to the king. "He demoralizes the soldiers who are left in this city, and all the people . . . He is not interested in the welfare of our people, but in their ruin."
> King Zedekiah answered, "He is in your power . . ."
> So they took Jeremiah and threw him into the cistern . . . which was in the quarters of the guard, letting him down with ropes.
> There was no water in the cistern, only mud, and Jeremiah sank into the mud. (Jeremiah 38:4–6)

✦  ✦  ✦

**3:52–54**

> Those who were my enemies without cause
> hunted me down like a bird;
>
> they stuck me down alive in the pit,
> and sealed me in with a stone.
>
> The waters flowed over my head,
> and I said, "I am lost!"

✦  ✦  ✦

Jeremiah was not to die in the pit; he was rescued.
Another—if possible, worse—fate loomed.
After the fall of Jerusalem, the prophet lingered amid the ruins for awhile: "And so he remained among the people"(39:14).

Finally, through a band of conspirators, he was forced into Egyptian exile. There, a very old tradition has it, he was murdered by his own countrymen. A life haunted by God, and a strangely befitting end.

✦  ✦  ✦

In the not-so-dry well, the story has it, Jeremiah is silent as Jonah in the whale's belly.

Our scene leaves him there. We shift to the dynamics of rescue:

> Now Ebed-melech, a courtier of the king's palace, heard that they had put Jeremiah in the cistern . . . .
>
> Ebed-melech said to the king, "My lord, these men have been at fault in all they have done to the prophet Jeremiah, casting him into the cistern. He will die of famine on the spot, for there is no more food in the city."
>
> Then the king ordered Ebed-melech to take three men along with him, and draw the prophet Jeremiah out of the cistern before he should die . . . (38:7–10)

✦  ✦  ✦

**3:55–57** In our poem, Jeremiah is given voice, and more—an altogether singular intervention.

Does the prophet plead for a miracle? He shall have something both more and less. An obscure courtier lets a lifeline down and down.

Miracle, magic, mystery? In a first act of our drama, it is as though God let down and down a rope, and drew someone, otherwise unknown (but chosen!)—drew this one from the selfishness, intrigues, and shifty self-interest of the imperial court.

He saves Jeremiah, and in so doing, is saved.

This someone is very nearly a no one—a black slave from Cush.

Says God: Now I have you, Ebed-melech!

✦  ✦  ✦

And on to act two: Take the rope in hand, save My prophet.

The ironies! To save a man condemned to death, God appoints a slave.

What follows is quite properly an act of God, no less so for issuing from a compassionate human:

> I called upon Your name, O God
> from the bottom of the pit;

You heard me call; "Let not Your ear
be deaf to my cry for help!"

You came to my aid when I called to You;
You said; "Have no fear!"

✦ ✦ ✦

One more episode concerns our Sudanese slave, and a comforting one. His magnificent, risky work of rescue is not forgotten.

Jerusalem has fallen. For a time, Jeremiah is immune from the decree of mass murder and exile.

And what of Ebed-melech? No such protection is offered him; he goes into hiding, his life at risk.

But neither God nor Jeremiah has forgotten.

In a marvelous reversal of roles, the original rescue is repeated. Now it is Jeremiah, at the behest of God, who deals out a lifeline to the slave:

"Have no fear!" was the word that came to the prophet in the pit. Now the same word envelops the slave, invites his confidence in God through Jeremiah.

In a ruthless time, a lovely, tender diminuendo:

. . . the word of God came to Jeremiah;

"Go, tell this to Ebed-melech";

"Behold, I am now fulfilling the words I spoke against this city, for evil and not for good; and this before your very eyes.

"But on that day I will rescue you," says God, "you shall not be handed over to the men of whom you are afraid; I will make certain that you escape and do not fall by the sword.

"Your life shall be spared as booty, because you trusted in Me," says God. (Jeremiah 39:15–18)

✦ ✦ ✦

**3:58–61** The cry for justice, unmoved by mercy, becomes a cry for vengeance. How fatefully easy the slide!

It moves ever so slowly, all but invisibly, across the landscape of a culture, like a dawn or twilight fog.

The Manhattan towers fell, wrecked, spilling humans like a debris. And the cry went up: "Give us justice!"

Then: "Avenge our dead!"

There followed the immense mobilization, a juggernaut across the world.

In the haystack, where, O where is that odious needle?

✦　✦　✦

> You defended me in mortal danger,
> You redeemed my life.

A fair enough beginning, a confession; a plenary favor has been conferred, evoking strong gratitude.

Then, a swift change of pace and mood.

Dwelt on, nursed, cozened, eclipsing the light—the memory of wrongs nudge one down and down, a ruinous change of soul.

That pit again: it becomes a home ground, a geography of soul. Where one is stuck. Where one resists all rescue.

✦　✦　✦

Poisoned memories take command. Tit for tat expands the Decalogue, God is drawn into the maelstrom of ambiguous (and not so ambiguous) purpose.

Revenge. The slide is underway.

Or the mind turns and turns on tormenting occasions, like meat on a spit:

> You see O God, how I am wronged;
> do me justice!

> You see all their vindictiveness,
> all their plots against me.

> You hear their insults, O God,
> all their designs against me.

✦　✦　✦

We ponder the words of the wronged one, we set down reflections that come to mind. And we are half ashamed—or more than half.

Truth told (tell it!) we too have been there, in the pit, on the spit. We know the mood that reaches for a weapon. Even for an imaginary weapon.

Reaches perhaps for the deadliest weapon of all; the tongue, and a bloodless phantasy of murder in the mind.

We too have said to our own soul; I am wronged, that is the truth of my life, the only truth. Darkness, be my light.

✦   ✦   ✦

At a gathering of peace folk on the west coast in the mid-sixties, one of those present (politically incorrect to be sure, a kind of unconstructed original), blurted this, out of the blue: "I think there is enough anger in this room to fuel the Vietnam War."

Almost four decades later, I remember what I took to be a salutary warning. No magic needle immunizes humans, whether peacemakers or others, against the poison that fuels great crime. In ancient Jerusalem, in today's New York.

✦   ✦   ✦

**3:62–63** Talk about obsessive! The mood feeds upon itself, it will not yield.

And there is alas, no interlocutor or mediator or friend at hand, to counsel, to mitigate, to say, "go slow"! A dour state of soul prevails, with no grammar of dissent.

Are these "foes" the poet's version of the friends of Job?

They haunt, they hang about indefinitely. Are they there in the flesh, are they airy phantoms of a mind that has lost its moorings?

A corrosive sourness creates its own presences and ominous "whispers."

> The whispered murmurings of my foes,
> against me all the day.
>
> Whether they sit or stand,
> see, I am their taunt song.

✦   ✦   ✦

**3:64–66** At length a prayer, forming a conclusion of the long central third chapter of Lamentations.  As might have been predicted, the prayer seeks requittal, a *quid pro quo*. Let the evil that has been dealt me, be dealt "the enemy."

The petition falls short of the gospel ideal, to be sure. Still, it is consonant with what went before—and to that degree, instructive.

✦   ✦   ✦

How often in our Lament, God has been subtly (or not so subtly) urged to put on a "mask of resemblance." The mood governs the prayer, something like this: If I seek mercy, show mercy by all means! But if darkness overtakes and resentment flares—let God play a kind of omnipotent ventriloquist to my leanings!

✦   ✦   ✦

The theme is perhaps ripe for a midrash. God, in Christ, might be thought to refuse the mask. Indeed, to insist on our unmasking:

> What I say to you is, offer no resistance to injury. When a person strikes you on the right cheek, turn and offer him the other.
>
> If anyone wants to go to law over your shirt, offer him your coat as well . . . .
>
> My command to you is; love your enemies, pray for your persecutors . . . (Matthew 5:39–40, 44)

✦   ✦   ✦

Something other, another way—how we long for its map, its method, in a world stuck in recrimination. Another than the ancient game, the fire perennially fanned, the acts of terror requited.

Something other than the random scorching of Afghanistan. Other than the fiery American clichès—bombing, bombing.

Something other indeed. Texts whose import was traced in the flesh and frame of the Crucified.

Texts dishonored in fiery crusade, pogrom, holocaust, invasion.

Texts contemned by Christian legerdemain, the "just war" follies hauled out yet again, a freak show of legitimacy, deranging ethicists and disciples, both.

✦   ✦   ✦

What of the Church? Let the Church play grand inquisitor, let this fiery, implacable personage indict Christ once again, proclaiming for all to hear, the mutual interests of church and state. Let him denounce the naive uselessness of nonviolence, and the supreme utility of the muscular "secular arm."

Raise it, the chastening, warning weapon. Let it fall and kill where required.

Let it fall, if it be required, on Christ Himself.

✦   ✦   ✦

And what of the Church?

Let the Church speak, not "the truth to power," but "the advantage of power redoubled." Let the Church announce that church and state are in

mutuality, that a "National Cathedral," a "just war theory," befit a pulpit
that proclaims no argument with the warmaking state.

An argument rather, with Christ.

✦   ✦   ✦

Conflict rages in the poet.

He approached the ruins of Jerusalem in chapter 3 as a threshing floor
of mercy or of retribution, the seat of God as Mercy or Requittal. The question: Who are You to us?

✦   ✦   ✦

Chapter 4 returns to the themes of chapters 1 and 2: personal loss, the
city as a stew of chaos and despair, of unmitigated suffering and near
extinction.

And the question: What is to become of us?

✦   ✦   ✦

**4:1–2** The poet is at a loss, except for sublimely apt metaphors that
bespeak loss itself.

He would have us see him, speechless, yet finding speech, a noble fic-
tion and irony. What is precious, and so rightly esteemed, has been reduced,
in an awful, literal sense—rendered.

"Gold" and "gems" are debased, despised, scattered abroad like offal.

But the precious metal and jewels yield to greater, more precious em-
blems—also lost, wasted. They gleam there in the rubble, noble metaphors,
humans—sons and daughters, discarded, "lives of no worth."

> How tarnished is the gold,
> how changed the noble metal;
>
> How the sacred stones lie strewn
> at every street corner.

The infamy named war. If this is the fate of children of war, what judgment lies on those who so dispose of children?

Let a human sense of altruism and compassion be extinguished—and
one is left an ethical monster.

Would the powerful who judge the children of enemies dispensable, so
dispose of their own children? What judgment lies on such, and those they
speak for?

✦   ✦   ✦

> Zion's precious sons,
> fine gold their counterpart,
>
> Now worth no more than earthen pots,
> made by the hands of a potter!

The pots too are endangered—in the frenzy, they may well be reduced to shards.

The poet is precise on every count and implication. In war, the children might be thought immune from the common fate.

Not at all, he implies.

He would have us look unflinchingly at the wars of our own times.

Ancient times, our own times, one and the same, an abomination.

We have seen in our Bible every crime consequent on war: betrayal of friends, hundred years' conflicts going nowhere, extermination mandated from on high, sieges laid against cities, their mothers resorting to cannibalism, helpless lepers caught between opposing armies, soldiers slaying their counterparts for entertainment of commanders. And so on, a history held up like an ensanguined mirror—of our own times.

And we are invited to ponder, and perhaps grow wise.

**4:3–5** War twists human affections about; the Bible tells stories of such aberrations, implacably. Warmth turns to inhuman cruelty, and this in the victors as well as the victimized.

Ours is precisely a poem "from below," its ambiance is the psychology and behavior of the destroyed—vis-à-vis the "enemy," as discussed above.

And toward one another, as here:

> Even the jackals bare their breasts
> and suckle their young.
>
> The daughter of my people has become as cruel
> as the ostrich of the desert.

A species of poetic license? Hard to sustain, that charge of "cruelty." What is the mother to do, whence is she to offer her milk?

The plight of the innocent abides:

> The tongue of the suckling cleaves
> to the roof of its mouth in thirst;
>
> The babes cry for food,
> there is no one to give to them.

✦  ✦  ✦

No one, today, "to give to them." No one, because no will do so.

Hunger is a worldwide scourge, and food is manipulated, withheld, or given, a political tool.

Yet as Isaiah insisted, only if justice is planted, will peace be sown:

> See, a king will reign justly,
> and princes will rule rightly.
> Each will be a shelter from the wind,
> a retreat from the rain.
>
> They will be like streams of water in a dry country,
> like the shade of a great rock in a parched land . . . .

Then there are the others, the dark rulers, war makers, bereft of compassion, condemning the innocent to death:

> The fool speaks foolishly,
> planning evil in his heart;
>
> how to do wickedness,
> to speak perversely against God,
>
> to let the hungry go empty,
> and the thirsty without drink.
>
> And the tricksters use wicked trickery,
> planning crimes;
>
> how to ruin the poor with lies,
> and the needy when they plead their case. (35:1–2, 6–7)

✦  ✦  ✦

*Terror*, in the lexicon of the superstate, is a polluted word. What greater terror than pitiless economic policies, than bombs falling and sanctions imposed? Today 1.3 billion humans live in absolute poverty—70 percent of these are women.

The violent death of some 3,000 Americans is a national tragedy. That 40 million die yearly from hunger and hunger-related causes is—a statistic.

Someone has anchored the number with a metaphor. Death from world hunger is like the crashing of 320 jumbo jets every day, half the passengers being children.

✦   ✦   ✦

Those accustomed to dainty foods
perish in the streets;

those brought up in purple
now cling to the ash heaps.

What crueler contrasts? Prosperity, all good things securely at hand. Then an unimaginably awful outcome.

Unimaginable that this befall ourselves, that we be victimized, disoriented, cast aside.

Unimaginable that this text, mourning an appalling event, be set down, as true, as historical—as not, say—the fate of our vassals, the world's offal (the Afghans, the Kosovites, the Guatemalans). But our own, our own . . .

✦   ✦   ✦

So grand was the hegemony of Solomon, the resources, luxuries, exotic foods and clothing, gold and silver, all together drawn in a vast net, home to Jerusalem from across the world.

Our possessions defined us. Our identity was cast in gold.

> The gold that Solomon received every year weighed 666 gold talents, in addition to what came from the Tarshish fleet, from the traffic of merchants, and from all the kings of Arabia and the governors of the country.

> The king had a large ivory throne made, and overlaid it with refined gold . . . Nothing like this was produced in any other kingdom.

> In addition, all king Solomon's drinking vessels were of gold, and all the utensils in the Forest of Lebanon were of pure gold. There was no silver, for in Solomon's time it was considered worthless . . .

> Once every three years, the fleet of Tarshish would come in with a cargo of gold, silver, ivory, apes and monkeys. . . .

> Each one brought his yearly tribute; silver or gold articles, garments, weapons, spices, horses and mules. (1 Kings 10:14–22, 25)

✦   ✦   ✦

Idols? The thought perhaps occurred but was easily dismissed—a desert tale, or the raving of a distempered Jeremiah.

The system was overbearing, excessive, throttling of just or compassionate governance.

And not to be forgotten: a formidable military machine must be created and maintained. How otherwise secure this "godly way of life" (as a like pride in possession is sanctified in our own day):

> Solomon collected chariots and drivers; he had 1,400 chariots and 12,000 drivers. These he allocated among the "chariot cities" and to the king's service in Jerusalem (1 Kings 10:26)

Canny Solomon! A line of defense was created, and permanent army outposts maintained. This, we are told, was an imperial innovation.

A flood tide of domestic luxury, a powerful military. Does it sound familiar?

No wonder, even apart from the judgment of God, the realm fell apart.

✦   ✦   ✦

Biblical memory is not dead, even amid the half dead.

Prosperity brushed the memories aside, rendered them somnolent, irrelevant, an old wives' tale.

Who imagined, in the heady days, the high noon of empire, that Jerusalem would one day be compared (better, compare itself!) to—Sodom!

Beyond conceiving. Why it was in the Jerusalem of David and Solomon that the fate of Sodom was set down. As a kind of shadow-tale, an instructive opposite, a city off there somewhere, a place of idolatry and vice and fiery consequence.

And this in contrast to—what, to whom?

To Jerusalem, and "a mighty fortress, our god": temple, priesthood, liturgy, sacrifice, torah, tradition. Also "gold, silver, ivory, apes and monkeys . . . garments, weapons, spices, horses and mules."

And not to forget, as stern rebuke against impudent interference: "chariots and drivers, allocated . . ."

✦   ✦   ✦

**4:6** God did not say it; we said it.

To our lips arises the unthinkable trope, the confession. We are reduced to this: no longer Jerusalemites, the prideful of earth, the envied of tourist

and pilgrim. Our towers have collapsed, a rubble smoking with the stench
of the dead.

Consequence freezes the bones. Consequence only? But what of crime?
If so, crime also. Write it down, irrevocable. We have become Sodomites.

> The punishment of the daughter of my people
> is greater than the penalty of Sodom
>
> which was overthrown in an instant
> without the turning of a hand.

✦   ✦   ✦

That last line, a twist of the blade. No human hand was turned against
Sodom:

> . . . God rained down sulpherous fire upon Sodom
> and Gomorrah . . . overthrew those cities and the whole
> Plain . . .
>
> Early the next morning Abraham went to the place
> where he had stood in God's presence. As he looked down
> toward Sodom and Gomorrah and the whole region of
> the Plain, he saw dense smoke over the land, rising like
> fumes from a furnace. (Genesis 19:24–25, 27–28)

✦   ✦   ✦

> over the land,
>
> rising
> like fumes
>
> from
> a
> furnace . . .

Dare we speak of poetic justice? For eight weeks the smoke arose from
the great towers of the World Trade Center.

Someone said: "It is a stench I haven't smelled since Vietnam."

✦   ✦   ✦

Against Jerusalem the mailed fist of a goy descends, a counter imperi-
alist moving his forces against the imperial "chosen."

Who have become unchosen indeed, and brought low in the dust.

**4:7–8** Fired in the memory of loss, all who were once comely stand in the mind, larger, more beautiful than in life. "Princes," symbols of nobility of spirit.

The psychology is subtle, true to experience. It is as though the hand of the poet reached out for reassurance, to touch a beloved face. "Are you truly there?"

No one. He encounters only a shadow, a riven ghost, a revenant from the dead. Everyone, everything precious is lost.

And shall these not be held the more precious for that?

Start with a gorgeous, lissome imagery, as though drawn from a "song of Songs," awesome color, beauty beyond price or reckoning:

> Brighter than snow were her princes,
> whiter than milk,
>
> more ruddy than coral,
> more precious than sapphire.

✦　✦　✦

Scarcely mortal that beauty, assurance and dignity in its royal setting, the streets and squares of imperial Jerusalem.

What has befallen?

"I will show you fear in a handful of dust." Bare survival, near death. As though someone, barely recognizable, barely on his feet, staggered out of a concentration camp.

A talisman—of that century or this. An Abel dealt with by Cain, women and children under air assault:

> Now their appearance is blacker than soot,
> they are unrecognized on the streets;
>
> their skin shrinks on their bones,
> as dry as wood.

✦　✦　✦

**4:9–10** Jerusalem is under siege, choices are narrowed to the vanishing point. Nobles, mothers, children—death admits of no options. Death is the common portion.

But wait. One has an unsweet choice as to means: the sword, or starvation.

There has come a day when the living envy the dead:

> Better for those who perish by the sword
> than for those who die of hunger;

> Why waste away, as though pierced through,
> lacking the fruits of the field!

✦   ✦   ✦

Have we supped full of horrors? Worse—among the mothers of stricken Jerusalem, cannibalism breaks out:

> The hands of compassionate women
> boiled their own children,
>
> to serve them as mourners' food
> in the downfall of the daughter of my people.

✦   ✦   ✦

Deuteronomy had envisioned it—war and exile. In the course of a lengthy diatribe, "the final words of Moses," a dire warning is issued. Serve God, or else!

The horror of the passage mounts, detail crowding detail—ruin, in Jerusalem and throughout the land:

> In hunger and thirst, nakedness and utter poverty, you
> will serve the enemies whom God will send against you
> . . . a nation that shows neither respect for the aged nor
> pity for the young . . .
>
> . . . until the great unscaleable walls you trust in,
> come tumbling down all over your land.

Then, a drawn out sentence, as though reluctant to close. A death sentence. A sentence like the to-fro of a knell of doom, its rope pulled by a berserker:

> The most refined and delicate woman among you, so
> delicate and refined that she would not venture to set the
> sole of her foot on the ground, will begrudge her beloved
> husband and her son and daughter, the afterbirth that
> issues from her womb and the infant she brings forth,
> when she secretly uses them for food, for want of any-
> thing else, in the straits of the siege to which your enemy
> will subject you in your communities. (28:48, 50, 56–57)

✦   ✦   ✦

**4:11–13** Away from specific horror. Return once more to attribution; it is inconceivable, absurd, that our utter ruin be also—arbitrary.

It bears repeating, the instruction must be plunged home, like nails in living flesh. Our downfall has an Author as well as a human provocation. Let us yield before the hard truth, bowing low before an outcome our sins have contrived:

> God has spent anger,
> poured out blazing wrath,
>
> has kindled fire in Zion
> that has consumed her foundations.

✦   ✦   ✦

Then a curious turn. By every worldly calculation, whether of friend or enemy, Jerusalem seemed impregnable. "The great unscaleable walls you trust in . . ." how then could these "come tumbling down"?

Calculations of a greater might prevailing over a lesser, are hardly to be thought infallible.

On a clear late summer day, year 2001, imperial suppositions were shattered. Awful events rushed in like supersonic jets: the "unscaleable walls," the World Trade Center, tumbled to ground, Ground Zero. Zero money, zero trade, zero "normalcy." Rubble, humans gone to rubbish.

Suppositions strong as dogma, ideology beyond question—"might makes right"—these tumbled.

✦   ✦   ✦

If this can happen, what may not happen? A proud, unquestioning people, battening on the marrow of creation, is invited to a new under-standing—or is prodded into fits and starts of rage.

A "why?" arises like a ghost from a grave, a disinterment of deeds. "Why are we so hated?"

For the first time, beyond adolescence, our motives and behavior are placed in question. Summon them, deal with them.

Or backward we are flung to blind, pitiless reprisal. Truth told, in the image of our tormenters.

Forward, backward, which way to go?

A young novelist (and a formidable moralist) from India, writes:

> . . . Who is Osama bin Laden really? Let me rephrase
> that. What is Osama bin Laden? He's America's family
> secret. He is the American president's dark doppelganger.

The savage twin of all that purports to be beautiful and civilized.

He has been sculpted from the spare rib of a world laid to waste by America's foreign policy; its gunboat diplomacy, its nuclear arsenal, its vulgarly stated policy of "full-spectrum dominance," its chilling disregard for non-American lives, its barbarous military interventions, its support for despotic and dictatorial regimes, its merciless economic agenda that has munched through the economies of poor countries like a cloud of locusts. Its marauding multinationals who are taking over the air we breathe, the ground we stand on, the water we drink, the thoughts we think . . .

Now Bush and bin Laden have even begun to borrow each other's rhetoric. Each refers to the other as "the head of the snake." Both invoke God and use the loose millenarian currency of good and evil as their terms of reference.

Both are engaged in unequivocal political crimes. Both are dangerously armed—one with the nuclear arsenal of the obscenely powerful, the other with the incandescent, destructive power of the utterly hopeless . . . (Arundhati Roy, "The Algebra of Infinite Justice," *The Guardian*, 9/27/01)

✦   ✦   ✦

Fierce as a flail on human flesh, the indictment falls, and against the least likely of all!

Who would have dreamed it, a stalking nightmare, even as the sun paused at high noon, the apogee of empire, and Jerusalem preened and gleamed, the apple of God's eye?

This, the horror. The sacred fell victim to the profane, as priests and prophets laid violent hands on their own:

> Because of the sins of her prophets
> and the crimes of her priests,
>
> who shed in her midst
> the blood of the just—

And of the mournful strophe, its divisions and conflicts, Jesus will compose a close midrash, a new lament for an old, tears drawn from tears:

O Jerusalem
Jerusalem

you slay the prophets
and stone those sent to you

how often have I longed
to gather your children

as a mother hen
collects her young

but you
refused Me! . . .

Your temple
will be abandoned . . . (Luke 13:34, 35)

And in His last, fateful entrance into Jerusalem, a prophecy more detailed and awful:

> Coming within sight of the city, He wept over it, and said; "If only you had known the path to peace this day; but you have completely lost it from view!
> "Days will come upon you when your enemies encircle you with a rampart, hem you in, and press you hard from every side.
> "They will wipe you out, you and the children within your walls, and leave not a stone upon a stone, because you did not know the time of your visitation."
> (Luke 19:41–44)

✦ ✦ ✦

**4:14–16** And the shame of renegade priests and prophets.

What is their fate? It is terrible. Let it be set down, as though in the ledger of Furies.

To the eye of the poet (at least in this mood), consequence follows closely on crime. Unmasked, a coven of Cains, those who betray their calling are shunned, jostled from pillar to post, welcome nowhere, not even among the goys.

They are spiritual lepers-at-large, they evoke disgust and revulsion:

> They staggered blindly in the streets,
> soiled with blood,

so that people could not touch
even their garments.

"Away you unclean," they cried to them,
"Away, away, do not draw near!"

If they left and wandered among the nations,
nowhere could they remain.

✦   ✦   ✦

Tables are turned, victimizers victimized, the once honored and steady, the classic insiders—now shunned, "undocumented," landless, at home nowhere, estranged from pity and welcome.

In a punishing encounter out of Genesis, the God of surprises confronts the fratricide Cain:

God then said;

"What have you done! Listen, your brother's blood cries out to Me from the soil!

"therefore you shall be banned from the soil that opened its mouth to receive your brother's blood from your hand. If you till the soil, it shall no longer give you produce . . ." (4:10–12)

✦   ✦   ✦

These latter-day Cains, let them not escape the judgment of heaven. The decree is as old as Genesis; shamefully and rightly it connects them with their lineage, the line sin has formed.

Are they not bastard sons of Cain, who slew his brother, and all unwitting, offered a definition of the crime of war—the slaying of a brother?

God speaks to Cain:

. . . "you shall become a restless wanderer upon the earth."

And let these discredited haters and killers suffer a like outcome:

God has dispersed them,
regards them no more;

does not receive the priests with favor,
nor show kindness to the elders.

✦  ✦  ✦

**4:17–19** Memory ventures back and back, a snare in hand. The poet recalls the bootless hope that preceded catastrophe. It rested on Egypt, and disastrously.

The diplomatic turn was derided by the Assyrians. Before the assault on Jerusalem, they send a delegation from king Sennacherib, undoubtedly to test the waters of resistance. This was their jibe, as recorded by Isaiah:

> On whom do you rely, that you rebel against me? This
> Egypt, the staff on which you rely, is in fact a broken reed
> which pierces the hand of anyone who leans on it . . .
> (36:5–6)

✦  ✦  ✦

Such aid was sought, looked for night and day as the siege neared, then was mounted in fury:

> Our eyes ever wasted away,
> looking in vain for aid;

The hope dissolved. Jerusalem fell, and the taunt of the enemy was verified:

> From our watchtower we watched
> for a nation that would not save us.

✦  ✦  ✦

Who but an eyewitness, dazed, walking the ruined squares, could report the thorough vandalism of the invaders?

Within the larger scenes of ruin, he offers nightmarish mini episodes. The city is taken. There follows a human roundup, as of cattle or horses:

> Men dogged our steps
> so that we could not walk in our streets.

> Our end drew near, and came;
> our time had expired.

✦  ✦  ✦

Starvation or the sword. And outside the walls, where to find refuge?

The nobles and artisans and priests set out on their trail of tears, reduced to a fleeing, chaotic crowd of refugees. Nature and season favored the victors.

No place to hide—those who fled were pursued and cornered, taken captive, bundled off like the others or slain on the spot:

> Our pursuers were swifter
> than eagles in air.
>
> They harassed us on the mountains,
> and waylaid us in the desert.

Modern poets too have suffered harshly. One among them writes ironically of loss and letting go. He knows whereof he writes—in occupied Poland he was fired from teaching, harassed, and forbidden publication.

He survived, to bear witness for others who underwent a fate worse than his; the voiceless, put to silence, put to death:

IF CHINA

> If China, then only the kind
> you wouldn't miss under the movers' shoes or the treads
>         of a tank;
> if a chair, then one that's not too comfortable, or
> you'll regret getting up and leaving;
> if clothes, then only what will fit in one suitcase;
> if books, then those you know by heart;
> if plans, then the ones you can give up
> when it comes time for the next move,
> to another street, another continent or epoch
> or world;
>
> Who told you you could settle in?
> who told you this or that would last forever?
> Didn't anyone tell you you'll never
> in the world
> feel at home here?

(Stanislaw Baranczak, *Selected Poems*. Evanston, IL: Triquarterly Books, Northwestern University Press, 1989)

✦  ✦  ✦

As these notes set down in winter of 2001, the bootless war in Afghanistan wears on. The refugees flee to the mountains, amid snowfall, misery, death for many.

These words of lament are written none the less in hope, that vagrant, fragile winter flower. Someday, after the technological bullies have had their day, the vast silence of the victims will end.

We shall hear the voices of the poets of Afghanistan, bearing witness, buoying our spirit—those who together with ourselves, have resisted and survived—and speak up.

## chapter five

# "To you also shall the cup be passed"
# (4:20–5:22)

**4:20–22** There was hope for awhile, we are told, even after the downfall of the city.

The hope was drastically curtailed, to be sure; Jerusalem was in ruins, the dread exile was underway. Still, for some eleven years, a kind of hope, constantly endangered, gradually diminishing, lived on.

Babylon, so the logic went, was not the entire world; there were other neighbors. (Those Edomites, no great friends, to be sure; and the Egyptians, who in the breach failed us . . .)

Still, could not a remnant, reduced to the sure, but surviving (the main issue after all), mingle among these and other tribes?

✦ ✦ ✦

The last hope is the least sure. By 587 CE, matters fell to pieces.

Matters named thus: sheer survival as a people.

Like storm-driven birds, wherever the winds landed us, we were exiles, pure and simple.

✦ ✦ ✦

Nonetheless, the poet turns to that interim, when hope flickered on, uncertain, a flame half quenched.

Nonetheless, let us hold the torch aloft, first as a tribute to the king, our king. May he prosper—or at least survive. For in his fate is enveloped our own—at least the fate of some of us.

And in an ecumenical spirit, we mingle the royal titles: Hebrew first, "the anointed," as befits. Then Egyptian, "breath of life," a nod to a powerful neighbor.

The titles are recalled with a twist, a pang of sorrow and regret.

The king too is doomed, another entry in the calculus of loss:

> The anointed one of God, our breath of life,
> was caught in their snares,

111

he in whose shadow we thought
we could live on among the nations.

✦  ✦  ✦

Are vain hopes better than none?

Those Edomites were immemorially at odds. They took advantage of
the chaos that followed on the disaster of 583, irritating, encroaching on
Juda. For this they won the unwelcome attention of the great prophets—
Isaiah, Jeremiah, Ezekiel united in denouncing their opportunism.

Among the chosen, the memory of Edomites was a bitter pill indeed.
Hadn't they, in the wilderness years after the Exodus, refused to allow great
Moses passage through their lands, forcing the wanderers to make a long,
arduous detour?

The rancor was ancient, and mutual to both parties. David had con-
quered and humiliated the Edomites.

✦  ✦  ✦

**4:21–22** No wonder then, this vexing, slippery neighbor enters the
lament. Edom also is a "daughter" of sorts, she is a partner in the crimes
that brought the chosen to grief.

Does she take wicked pleasure in the ruin of her rival? She does.

But wait. God is patient, with the goys as with the chosen.

Meantime, the cup of gall is seemingly bottomless. Jerusalem, for all
its bitter quaffing, has not drunk to the lees.   Let the cup be passed to
Edom, of "the land of Uz" (interestingly specified here as the land of Job. Is
a hint placed in the text, of sorrow impending?)

In any case, let this misfortunate, estranged "daughter," be paired with
the daughter of Jerusalem. Let the name Edom be set down in the ledger of
crime and consequence:

> Though you rejoice and are glad, O daughter Edom,
> you who dwell in the land of Uz,
>
> to you also shall the cup be passed;
> you shall become drunk and naked.

✦  ✦  ✦

Edom sticks in the poet's craw. Misfortunate, one takes a scurvy glee
amid a fraternity of misfortune. Partners welcome!

So the theme here: daughter Zion suffers incalculable losses, to be sure.
But what of daughter Edom, what portends for her?

Let the poet for the moment play prophet:

Your chastisement is completed, O daughter Zion,
God will not prolong your exile;

But your wickedness, O daughter Edom, God will punish,
will lay bare your sins.

✦ ✦ ✦

**5:1–6** The mood swings once more, back to the earlier lament and supplication. The God who sees all, surely sees ourselves, reduced to near nothing.

Dazed, grief-stricken, we cannot so much as comprehend our plight, its "why."

We pray then. You who have named Yourself Mother, Father, Lover, Friend—please regard our plight. Surely You cannot but be moved, and intercede.

(But God can indeed remain unmoved, this God who at times so resembles the sovereign automaton of the scholastics, the "Unmoved Mover."

(To his chagrin and anger, Job too must lend ear to a like version, as his friends windily proclaim their God, a rigorous Weigher of Those Found Wanting.

(Need it be added, the friends had in view a version of humans as well, including a disdainful version of Job—and with noses held high, smug self-approval as well!)

✦ ✦ ✦

The tone of the prayer that follows, recalls the long plaint of Job, as well as the ambient realities that so vex him—the condescending "explanations" of his friends, the obtuse wall of the world's events, the withholding, silent God.

Still, in our Lamentation, we note an astonishing development, as the grief of Job issues from the lips of an entire people.

✦ ✦ ✦

A last-ditch prayer, laved in a kind of wonderment. In shock, in near despair, we lorn ones, once the apple of God's eye, cannot take in the crushing depth of our predicament.

Still, this is left to us: prayer. May You supply for our dire lack, for the memory and sight which fail us.

Let us confess. Long before disaster struck, we were dis-membered, spiritually. And afterward, we are blinded as to cause and outcome.

This be a first mercy on our behalf. What we are incapable of, You please do on our behalf. "Remember," and "see."

Remember O God, what has befallen us,
look and see our disgrace. (5:1)

Would this be conceivable—that our God could be less compassionate than ourselves, the work of God's hands? Has not God urged repeatedly through the prophets, mercy toward "widows and orphans and strangers at the gate"?

This is plain, brute fact. What we once beheld, mercifully or otherwise—that we have become. We are the "strangers . . . foreigners . . . orphans . . . fatherless . . . widowed . . ."

Bonds that once held close in blood or friendship are sundered.

Behold the once powerful, the citizens of empire; we are the outsiders, the vulnerable. We must stretch out our hands to others (above all, to Another!)

✦  ✦  ✦

As these notes are set down, events slide into incoherence and loss, a reversal of status, of who a people are, what they may hope for, what escapes their grasp: Palestinians, Afghans—as formerly South Africans, Central Americans, Kosovites, the Northern Irish, the children of Iraq. And so on, that litany of loss.

On whom must responsibility for the plight of entire peoples be placed?

Massive crimes of war violate the human measure. Nothing that once weighed strongly applies—neither contract nor laws of inheritance nor simple honor nor respect for age or innocence nor the protection of non-combatants.

Roles (and rules!) shift, existence is shuffled about like a deck of cards in the hands of a prestidigitator.

Must some win, must others lose and lose, for a lifetime, for generations? Is this the game, is the metaphor apt to good sense—winners, losers?

And shall the God of the Bible not prove an honest player?

✦  ✦  ✦

If honest, what of this?

Our inherited lands have been turned over to strangers,
our homes to foreigners.

We have become orphans, fatherless;
widowed are our mothers. (5:2–3)

✦  ✦  ✦

Hewers of wood, drawers of water. For generations, this defined those enslaved in Egypt. Then from slaves we became nomads, set free by Your providence. Then, then. Imperial instincts beckoned— despite the warnings of prophet Samuel, we would have a king "like the nations."

With a vengeance, kings were ours. Saul, David, Solomon, Hezekiah, the others. We stood in the high noon of empire, everything turned to gold: temple, palace, soaring economy and invincible armies, chariots and gold ingots and trade treaties and world prestige. Ours, ours, ours.

What our memories cherished, what liturgies and ceremonies summoned with a leap of heart's gratitude, how You snatched us from ruin, feeding us from high heaven—the memories fell to near nothing, swept into mindlessness before an onslaught of appetite and accumulation. Make way for the rain of gold, for military might!

We had arrived. And we were nowhere.

Then tragedy, the fall of the topless towers. The empire fell about our ears.

We held out a beggar's bowl and whimpered. We became what our wars, our greed, once pocked the world with—those "others," creditors, bankrupts, "widows and orphans and strangers at the gate."

What does God have in store, what does a text heavy with reversal of fortune teach us? Can it be that we Americans, the high and mighty of the world, will one day become landless refugees, Afghans or Iraqis or Guatemalans or Kosovos or Colombian peasants, the "we" become "they," the "ours" theirs, as we seek a handout at the portal where Dives gluts and forgets?

> The water we drink we must buy,
> for our own wood we must pay. (5:4)

A hideous world arises, our own. A warmaking superstate controls markets and resources. Oil is a totem, worth its weight in blood.

With an economic sword, humanity is divided down the middle.

No, not the "middle." Into the many, the enslaved, and the favored few, who drive hard bargains. A ramshackle world, nailed together in one night. A world like a gigantic sweatshop—those who sweat, and those who shop.

Or a slave market, money driven.

The state represents all the autocratic, arbitrary, coercive, belligerent forces within a social group, it is a sort of complexus of everything most distasteful in the modern, free, creative spirit, the feeling of life, liberty and the pursuit of happiness.

War is the health of the State. Only when the State is at war, does the modern society function with the unity of sentiment, simple, uncritical, patriotic devotion, cooperation of services which have always been the ideal of the State lover. (Randolph Bourne, "The Radical Will," quoted in a review in the *Catholic Worker,* November 2001)

✦   ✦   ✦

On our neck is the yoke of those who drive us,
We are worn out, but are allowed no rest. (5:5)

✦   ✦   ✦

The "we" of the text is vast, and implies, as suggested, that social, economic, and religious roles have inexplicably been spun about.

Darkness descends, a night of wrestling with angels and demons, a rough and tumble history.

And a God, enraged with the follies of those who lay a mailed hand on lands and markets and human lives—and heaven. Ourselves.

✦   ✦   ✦

In the course of American hegemony (those phrases trippingly on the tongue: "our way of life . . . our national interests . . . globalization . . . trickle down economics . . . just war theory . . .") more than 200 years of imperial ascendancy, up to say, mid morning of September 11, 2001— whose nightmare would have conjured this?

White House to Pentagon to World Trade Center, the fabric of supposition, prosperity, confidence, religion, was ripped like a rotten arras. The president hid out, the towers fell, the living were catapulted into space, the military sanctum was brutally breached.

And this, three months later:

AT THE PIT, A NIGHT SHIFT TO NUMB THE
BODY AND SOUL

"The winter days are long and dark and cold," Eddie Reinle said . . . "they're fourteen-and-a-half-hour days

now. Maybe in the summer I'll get more sleep, if I live
that long."

There is no extra money for working the night shift,
though there are extra physical and psychological chal-
lenges. There are the strained marriages, the spotty eyes
from the floodlights, the cold and wind . . .

The workers . . . do not count their success in metal or
tonnage, but in bodies. At 6 p.m. Friday, the work stops,
two uniformed bodies are found. They are firefighters, their
remains are bagged and covered with a flag and taken
out of the pit through a double column of mudstained
firefighters. A salute is given, a prayer offered and finally
they are driven away to the temporary morgue . . .

When the bodies are gone, the work resumes. . . . The
smells are of burning wiring, dankness from the subway
tunnels and the sweet, acrid, cherry-like smell of death . . .
(*New York Times*, 12/10/01)

✦  ✦  ✦

Multiply the eerie scene a thousandfold across the world. Create a new
composition of place; the mountains of Afghanistan, winter descending,
multitudes of refugees fleeing the bombers, food and shelter and medical
help in short supply—or no supply at all.

The American media have offered months of loving tribute to each of
those who fell in the burning towers. But the dead of Afghanistan, those
who died under the bombs or in the refugee camps, are neither counted
nor named.

During the experience of years spent in the debris of
modern war, I became aware of a dread reality, the fact
that modern war does not merely interrupt, but reverses,
every Work of Mercy. (Eileen Egan, quoted in *Catholic
Worker*, December 2001)

✦  ✦  ✦

Meantime, in November of '01, the Catholic bishops held their annual
meeting in Washington. The U.S. was bombing Afghanistan night and
day. In the winter snow, more than 7 million impoverished peasants of
that country, displaced by air assaults, had fled to the mountains.

Meantime, the bishops hosted a Mass "for peace." An admiral from
the Pentagon read from Scriptures. Then the outgoing president of the
bishops' conference read from the Sermon on the Mount—the urgent plea

of Jesus that His disciples love their enemies and react with hatred toward none.

After the gospel reading, the bishop made clear his approval of the war in Afghanistan. And the day following, the newly elected bishop president repeated official approval of the war.

> To bomb an innocent people, an illiterate people, a destitute people into tent cities on foreign borders— babies in their bellies and old people on their backs—is obscene.
>
> To starve out a half million people tonight, another three million soon, seven million—the entire population of New York City by the end of winter . . . is to shift the moral question away from terrorism to the "integrity" of bombing. (Sr. Joan Chittister, OSB, quoted in *National Catholic Reporter,* January 2002)

Catastrophe makes strange bedfellows.

Another image; tables are turned quite literally on traditional commensalism.

When victuals fall desperately short, who comes forward compassionately? What of the former imperial darlings and their gourmet appetites? Are the chosen reverting to the wilderness years and plaints for the fleshpots of Egypt? Will the God who granted quail and manna in the wilderness create new miracles of plenty?

God will not. Turn elsewhere is the only message from the blank heavens.

After the horrid fact, everything familiar and taken for granted, is now "former." Turn to former enemies; for the uneasy present, count them reluctant friends. You could do worse.

To the victors belong the spoils. Eat the bread of humiliation.

Food too is tainted; it has become a tool of domination, dispensed or withheld in accord with "national interest."

Translate, as per Mr. Bush: "those not with us are against us."

Translate the Delphic dictum, this perhaps: "Let many die, if need be, that a few may prosper."

To Egypt we submitted
And to Assyria, to fill our need of bread. (5:6)

✦   ✦   ✦

**5:7–8** Memory is an open wound. The wound is the voice of the body, an only word: pain. Return to it, as though turning a blade in the flesh. The hurt festers away, a fever rises.

Were we once prosperous, did we hold our heads high among the nations? Delusion, fool's gold.

Or summon the memory of joy. It becomes a further onslaught, high tide in a sea of pain.

Nothing new under the sun. Hope stops here.

✦   ✦   ✦

Despair takes this form; we must pay and pay for the sins of ancestors. (The sins also are our own, as admitted elsewhere, but this is a feverish night, and an obsessive ghost is abroad).

Our fathers who sinned, are no more;
but we bear their guilt.

Is it true, is it untrue, this sense of tainted blood, of a wasting generational illness, of soul sagging away from uprightness?

Untrue! The diagnosis has been abrogated by the healer Jeremiah:

In those days, they shall no longer say;

"the fathers ate unripe grapes,
and the children's teeth are set on edge."

But through one's own fault only
shall anyone die;

the teeth of the one
who eats the unripe grapes
will be set on edge. (31:29–30)

✦   ✦   ✦

Let the words stand, as such words will. They may sustain in normal times.

But there are other words for abnormal times. And these prevail, for they tell of a wound. It is night and memory bleeds.

The ghost named guilt, fantastic, larger than life, walks the cave of the mind.

✦  ✦  ✦

Counterpoint, and yet another humiliation. We who once ruled others, are now enslaved; once the lords of history, behold us, lorded over.

And, over us, "slaves," or "servants of the ruler," a Hebraism, of double meaning. And for ourselves, a double jeopardy.

Would that we dwelt in Babylon and could take our chances on an absolute (but perhaps enlightened) monarch! Pity us in limbo, reminded daily of former grandeur, subject to a corrupt overlord, imposed on us by a distant, indifferent king.

An awesome irony—only the free can be so pained, knowing their plight, summoning their predicament, two-cents plain:

> Slaves rule over us;
> there is no one to rescue us from their hands.

✦  ✦  ✦

**5:9–10** A humiliating question arises, like a gorgon from a nightmare. How are we to survive in a new wilderness?

No need to add—among the pampered citizens of Solomon's empire, the question never arose. It was the "others," the slaves and forced laborers and hoplites—it was they whose prospects were chancy, who might survive or might not.

But we were the darlings of accumulation and surfeit. The chronicler glories in the telling, as a culture took its cue from the sun king: wealth, loot, the lucky pitch.

And of the king it was written:

> King Solomon made two hundred shields of beaten gold . . . and three hundred bucklers of beaten gold. . . . The king also had a large ivory throne made, and overlaid it with refined gold . . . Nothing like this was produced in any other kingdom . . . (1 Kings 10:16–19)

✦  ✦  ✦

To be sure, in times past, survival was an issue indeed—the wilderness years. Then, God must intervene. Food fell from heaven in a benign storm.

No surfeit, no lack—heaven-honored creation by entering its process, blessing it, turning the desert into a momentary garden of plenty:

> In the morning, a dew lay all about the camp, and
> when the dew evaporated, there on the surface of the desert
> were fine flakes like hoarfrost on the ground.
> On seeing it, the Israelites asked one another, "What
> is this?," for they did not know what it was. But Moses
> told them, "this is the bread which God has given you to
> eat." (Exodus 16:13–15)

✦  ✦  ✦

In due time, the food from heaven melted like a snowfall in spring.
The economics of empire swamped the economics of heaven. The social
appetite grew sophisticated, choosy. As the king, so the court and its nobles.

They sailed the seven seas in search of world markets, an early instance of the "globalization" of trade:

> The gold that Solomon received every year weighed
> six hundred and sixty-six gold talents, in addition to what
> came from the Tarshish fleet, from the traffic of merchants,
> and from all the kings of Arabia and the governors of the
> country . . . .
> Each one brought his yearly tribute; silver or gold ar-
> ticles, garments, weapons, spices, horses and mules . . .
> (1 Kings 10:14–15, 25)

Imperial logic demanded a military force. How otherwise protect the
trade routes, the holy city, the vast loot, and those in possession?
So:

> Solomon collected chariots and drivers. He had one
> thousand four hundred chariots and twelve thousand driv-
> ers.
> These he allocated among the chariot cities and to
> the king's service in Jerusalem. (1 Kings 10:26)

✦  ✦  ✦

Memory is a free fall. The people are stricken to ground, defeated, bewildered wanderers under a desert sun.
Lament, make do:

> At peril of our lives, we bring in our sustenance
> in face of the desert heat . . . (5:9)

✦   ✦   ✦

Once they ate their fill. In a verse teeming with excess, the account was kept;

> Solomon's supplies for each day were thirty kors of fine flour, sixty kors of meal, ten fatted oxen, twenty pasture-fed oxen, and a hundred sheep, not counting harts, gazelles, roebucks and fatted fowl. (1 Kings 5:2)

✦   ✦   ✦

Lament. Hunger consumes us, and no relief from heaven or earth with the searing blasts of famine.

✦   ✦   ✦

> For the first time since the United States went to war in Afghanistan, food was delivered at a sprawling refugee camp in Bagh-i-Shirkat near Kunduz, where thousands of families huddled in freezing mud and filth, desperately awaiting nourishment, warm clothing and medical attention.
>
> In that one camp alone, more than 175 refugees, most of them children, have died in the past two months. (*New York Times*, 12/11/01)

✦   ✦   ✦

**5:11** The ancient disaster was random, and horridly thorough. It spared no one.

That our soldiers and those of the attacker died, is no news at all, and is not so much as recorded here.

Set down rather is an instance of a brutal clichè of our lifetime. We call it total war. For the defeated, it translates simply, brutally: doom. No one is spared or exempt, a once valid excusing cause is blasted to dust.

✦   ✦   ✦

The irony is appalling, and true. Rules governing a "just war" hold firm—in peacetime.

The stipulations are taught in universities and seminaries. Infants are to be protected, and the aged, women, the ill, those ignorant or innocent of the issues at stake.

Naive, abstract, unverifiable, the rules ignore the heat and torment of

the moment. The nation is at war; this is brute fact. Shall there be prattle
of rules of civilized combat?

First to the fate of women.

Look to it, warriors and war makers—in our lament, women are the
first to fall. They are the prime and horrid target, the prey of war as such.

Their shame becomes (though is left unstated in the poem), a judgment against the victors:

> The women in Zion were ravished by the enemy,
> the maidens in the city of Judah.

✦  ✦  ✦

But, but. War turns all theories, even the most virtuous, to smoke. Neigh-
borhoods are kindled, afire. People of any age or condition stagger about
under the guns, the bombs.

What is their offense, why are they disposed of? They get in the way of
a clean outcome, that is the sum of it. Their offense is—existence.

Kill them, civilians. In large numbers. Such things happen. They are
not exceptional; they are the random rule of the kingdom of chaos.

✦  ✦  ✦

The above speak of mischance or distraction or venom, a litany bearing disaster to the hapless.

Still, a question remains: what of the victors, what gifts from the hand
of Mars reward them?

Ambiguous gifts, at the least. A solider conviction, like the callous on a
warrior's hand, that battle is the sure path to glory, to self-justification, to
the admiration of peers and of women. In sum, to an immortality of sorts.

Also to medals, loot, and given skill and good luck, a secure retire-
ment.

✦  ✦  ✦

**5:12** War, the great leveler, in more senses than one.

War permits two categories of humans, two only: warrior and vanquished. Or another duet: survivors and the dead.

You were once somebody, a personage of note? War is declared. All
former honors, achievements, emoluments are canceled. You are a near
nobody—or worse, an enemy, someone to be removed from the world:

> Princes were gibbeted by them,
> elders shown no respect.

✦ ✦ ✦

**5:13** In time of peace, slaves and forced laborers were at hand, "drawers of water and hewers of wood." Theirs was judged a worthy, even a holy task—they built the temple and the palace of Solomon, maintained the great houses of noble families.

"Worthy, holy task?" An easy, distant consecration.

"Princes . . . elders . . ." Ours were higher tasks—planning, overseeing. We gave orders, watched half distracted, as others staggered about, bent under burdens we never carried, not for an hour.

We would come to know—first hand, that "worthy, holy task."

And we would describe it differently, with a muttered curse:

> The youths carry the millstones,
> boys stagger under their load of wood.

✦ ✦ ✦

**5:14** Seven gates of the holy city! Within each, open space was easily converted into a court, an agora, a public market, a gathering place of elders and officials. There too, transactions requiring witnesses were enacted.

There strangers were honored and hospitality offered, as in the story of the angelic visitors whom Lot greets at the gates of Sodom (Genesis 19:1 ff).

✦ ✦ ✦

Gates of glory, of power, of domination and conquest. And holy places as well, declared in the spontaneous cry of Jacob, "the abode of God and the gate of heaven!" (Genesis 28:17)

A rich, metaphoric space.

✦ ✦ ✦

Not to be wondered, Jesus, master of images, draws on it. Two gates are contrasted—the small, which accommodates only pedestrians, and the main, open to vehicles.

Illustration yields with ease to moral instruction:

> Enter through the narrow gate. The gate that leads to damnation is wide, the road is clear, and many choose to travel it.
>
> But how narrow is the gate that leads to life, how rough the road, and how few there are who find it! (Matthew 8:13–14)

✦  ✦  ✦

Much to-do, in sum, surrounds a rich and complex image.

But in our text it is summoned only as symbol of abandonment, emptiness. The gates have lost their power of evocation—no freedom, conviviality, decree, commerce, common life. The bustling center of the city, where music and human voices made merry, made solemn, made bargaining—is silent.

The silence signifies the death of a culture. Behold the ghastly triumph of war:

> The old men have abandoned the gate,
> the young men their music.

✦  ✦  ✦

**5:15–18** Herewith, as memory scalds anew, another mood (but surely the same?) *dulce vita,* those days of wine and roses, are vanished. What remains is a bitter lees, a cup of ecstasy turned to gall.

And our grief, awful as it is, allows a truth to emerge.

We who endure the end cannot summon ancestors to the bar. No, we acknowledge cause and consequence. It is we who have sinned, have brought the city tumbling about our heads:

> The joy of our hearts has ceased,
> our dance has turned into mourning.
>
> Garlands have fallen from our heads;
> woe to us, for we have sinned.

Grief is localized, an anchor plunged in the bitter waters of the heart. One place we mourn, no other:

> Over this our hearts are sick,
> at this our eyes grow dim;
>
> that mount Zion should be desolate,
> with jackals roaming there!

✦  ✦  ✦

The poetry has a life and rhythm of its own. It leans strongly on announcement, description, image upon image of desolation, within the soul and the social body.

Now and again images of loss are interrupted—the heart cries out in anguished prayer: this is too much, grant relief!

✦    ✦    ✦

**5:19–22** So we come to the majestic ending of Lamentations. Faith in God is the final word, intact—though like the holy city, battered.

A passing bell rings somberly: "it tolls for thee." The familiar shape of life—social, political, economic, religious—as known and loved, has fallen to a "once was," ended. Period.

The nobles fall to knee, and lower—faces against the earth, people mourn. A glorious scroll sighs as it is closed, thrice sealed, a blurred text of history.

The proud Jerusalemites, nobles, princes, bureaucrats, priests, artists— one and all they are fallen to vassals, slaves, exiles.

Or they die, and the corpses sprawl about, unburied.

✦    ✦    ✦

This opaque God, this Flail and Reaper, Judge and Prosecutor, nonetheless must be acknowledged. Faith demands it, faith pronounces it. Brought low, counting for little or nothing on the scales of this world (or for that matter, another world), the exiles touch the heart of faith.

Is the heart cold, stilled? Not altogether.

The beat is slowed. Confess. We have sinned, have comported ourselves like "the nations." Despite Moses and Samuel and the great prophets and martyrs, we have lusted after the gods of empire and made of the Temple an idolatrous sanctuary. We have waged horrid wars, defrauded, lied, betrayed, despised (even as our wars created) "widows and orphans and strangers at the gate."

✦    ✦    ✦

Return, return; in Lamentations the great Return from Babylon is prefigured. You shall return; in grief rather than hatred or recrimination, the Promise holds firm.

Lamentation enters the rhythm of life. It becomes an annual ritual; in prayer and fasting and mourning, we recall the mercy—and the mercilessness—of our God.

Let us return to our God; so doing, we resolutely return to ourselves, to our tradition, to the truth of life.

Let up set foot on the right, unerring way, a path of tears, but of salvation as well, eyes fixed on the prize.

✦    ✦    ✦

In our end is our beginning. We who suffer breathe deep and name God anew, borrowing the words of our great mentors:

> You, O God, are enthroned forever;
> Your throne stands from age to age.

Start with that, a direct address: "You." We do not plead with a phantom.

And let the language be a grandiose, compelling decor, a throne room, timeless. (Time will be honored later). "Forever . . . throne . . ." twice repeated, the praise driven home like bronze spikes securing a plaque of gold. Inscribed: "You."

Acknowledgment too, by way of implication. Something daringly simple, this confession. Only God is God.

Thus are horrific wrongs in the mind set to rights, like ingots plunged in fire and straightened.

Confess. We have been idolaters, in the sanctuary and on the battlefield.

Our Temple harbored in dark corners, secret worshippers of the gods of death.

Ezekiel was shown the horror.

Then, in a disdainful show of majesty, God abandoned the Temple, left the polluted sanctuary to idols and idolaters.

In the world too we played god, in demonic spasms of violence and pride. Wars declare our vile intention—superhuman stature, mastery of life and death.

Ancestors wrought the Fall—our plundering and despoiling of creation are its consequence.

Confess. We have trespassed on the domain of God. Like one-eyed giants we have crossed the boundaries of the forbidden.

Saul and David and Solomon may have uttered such words as end our book. But the prayers were tainted with madness and greed and the brutal scramble of ambition, as war upon war turned to jihad.

The will of the god! we cried. It was self-will hypostatized.

The holy city fell. And we survivors, at the end of our resources, stand chastened.

Creation is a wilderness, heartless, voiceless.

God too has become a question.

If God be a Question—then question God, in the majestic tradition of Job or Jeremiah.

Let our prayer match (with what pain), the wound of life, the predicament of the one (or the many) who so entreats:

> Why then, should You forget us,
> abandon us for so long a time?

✦  ✦  ✦

Now time also has its due. The God of eternity is summoned, questioned. The God who from eternity remembers, in time forgets.

Or so it is adduced, as God is sharply reminded, rebuked even.

God, accused?

This is a strange, venturesome, even dangerous religion—biblical religion.

✦  ✦  ✦

Strange too, and instructive, the victors, those who brought destruction and slavery, have nothing to say. They stand outside the scroll, except by way of derision or judgment.

Our protagonists are—the victims.

And these seek a hearing. They are scandalized, angered by the silence of God.

Why the wailing, why this talk of "forgetting . . . abandoning," except that we knew otherwise? Our stories of Exodus tell of it; once, God remembered, God cherished.

What a history is ours! Let it be summoned—predilection, covenant, wedding, friendship, sexual ecstasy, maternal cherishing, and holding close.

All such images being true, shall God now turn to stone, turn a stony ear to our plight?

God shall not. Or if so, God shall (so to speak) hear from us!

✦  ✦  ✦

The preceding was preliminary, a verbal decor. Now to the petition itself, the pith perhaps of the book. And how simply put, deceptively so, and with what deftness, what genius.

Let us take it slowly, mindfully, word by word:

Lead us back to You O God, that we may be restored . . .

✦　✦　✦

A theology of grace starts with a theology of sin. We have gone will-fully, repeatedly, astray—in wilderness first, then in temple and palace and market and home and battlefield.

Our sin, our twisted choices, invariably favored appetite and ego, vio-lence and greed.

You, knowing us, know all this.

You, knowing Yourself, know something more—infinitely more; manna in the wilderness, waters struck from rock. Mercy, patience, compassion.

We were gone astray. Only You can "lead us back."

And You will initiate the restoration and return. The *magnalia Dei,* the "great works of God," will be recorded, though not in this book, not in our lifetime. In promise and prospect.

✦　✦　✦

The petition continues:

Is this an echo of the wilderness years, of longing for the savory flesh-pots of slavery?

Or perhaps the plaint implies a nostalgic glance, over the shoulder so to speak, to the Solomonic days of wine and roses?

Or is something else at work? Do the exiles long for the thunderous words of prophets, the truth of God? Long to become once more a commu-nity of faith, ethically alert, passionately concerned for the "widows and orphans and strangers at the gate?"

✦　✦　✦

And if prophets were granted us, even in Babylon (as they were), would we not respond with a better, far more respectful hearing?

Through our travails grown apt for truth—we would, we would.

✦　✦　✦

Memories have stirred, awfully, at times hopefully. And the future has loomed, like a mountain that must be uprooted and removed from place, if the hegira is to go on.

And finally, inexorably—our plight must be faced; this unmediated, unrelieved catastrophe. Deprived and despised as we are, we must some-how walk through the day, toward a tomorrow whose other name is also—disaster.

And You have decreed this, allowed this, brought it to pass, this awful "now."

You witness it, a phalanx of staves laid on the backs of slaves, belaboring us hour upon hour.

The truth, which cannot be borne, and must be borne:

> For now, You have indeed rejected us,
> and in full measure turned Your wrath against us.

✦   ✦   ✦

NAB, GNB, NAS, RSV, all versions end here. But JPS prefers to echo once more, verse 22. Thus, one thinks, in a dying fall to summon hope:

> Take us back, O God, to Yourself.
> And let us come back.
> Renew our days as of old!